How to Fix Anxious and Avoidant Attachment Styles

The Ultimate Guide to Achieving Emotional Balance and Breaking Free from Anxiety to Security

BY

Rachel Keller

Table of Contents

Introduction

Understanding attachment styles is a crucial element in unraveling the complexities of human relationships. Attachment theory, which originated from the work of British psychologist John Bowlby, explores how early interactions with caregivers shape our expectations and behaviors in relationships throughout life. These early bonds set the foundation for how we connect with others, how we perceive love, and how we navigate intimacy and conflict. The significance of attachment styles extends far beyond childhood, influencing our adult relationships in profound and often unconscious ways. By exploring and understanding these styles, individuals can gain valuable insights into their relationship patterns, enhance their emotional intelligence, and foster healthier, more secure connections with others.

Attachment styles are generally categorized into four types: secure, anxious, avoidant, and disorganized. While a secure attachment style is associated with healthy, balanced relationships, the other three are considered insecure and can lead to difficulties in forming and maintaining healthy relationships. The anxious attachment style is characterized by a deep fear of abandonment and a constant need for reassurance, often leading to clinginess and dependency. On the other hand, the avoidant attachment style is marked by a strong desire for independence and self-reliance, often resulting in emotional distance and reluctance to form close bonds. Disorganized attachment, a less common but highly complex style, combines elements of both anxious and avoidant behaviors and is often linked to unresolved trauma. Understanding these attachment styles, particularly the anxious and avoidant types, is essential for those who seek to improve their relational dynamics and achieve emotional balance.

Why Understanding Attachment Styles Matters

The significance of understanding attachment styles cannot be overstated, as they play a pivotal role in shaping our emotional and psychological well-being. Attachment styles influence how we view ourselves, perceive others, and interact with the world around us. For instance, individuals with a secure attachment style typically have a positive self-image and a healthy view of others, leading to balanced and fulfilling relationships. They are comfortable with intimacy, trust others, and can effectively manage conflict. In contrast, those with insecure attachment styles may struggle with self-esteem issues, have difficulties trusting others, and may either fear intimacy or become overly dependent on their partners.

Understanding one's attachment style is a powerful tool for personal growth and relationship improvement. It provides insight into the underlying causes of relationship challenges and offers a roadmap for healing and change. By recognizing the patterns associated with anxious or avoidant attachment, individuals can begin to address the root causes of their relational difficulties, such as fear of abandonment, avoidance of emotional intimacy, or difficulty in expressing needs and desires. This self-awareness is the first step toward breaking unhealthy patterns and cultivating healthier, more secure relationships.

Moreover, understanding attachment styles is essential for fostering empathy and compassion in relationships. When individuals understand their own attachment style and that of their partners, they can better appreciate each other's emotional needs and responses. This awareness can lead to more effective communication, reduced conflict, and a deeper emotional connection. For example, an individual with an avoidant attachment style may struggle to express emotions, but understanding this as a defense mechanism rather than a lack of care can help their partner approach the situation with patience and understanding. In this way, understanding attachment styles not only benefits individuals but also enhances the quality of their relationships.

How Attachment Styles Impact Your Relationships

Attachment styles have a profound impact on how relationships are formed, maintained, and even dissolved. They influence everything from how individuals choose their partners to how they handle conflict and express love. For example, an individual with an anxious attachment style may find themselves drawn to partners who are emotionally distant or unavailable, subconsciously seeking to resolve their deep-seated fears of abandonment. However, this often leads to a cycle of insecurity and distress, as their need for constant reassurance clashes with their partner's desire for independence.

In relationships, those with an anxious attachment style often exhibit behaviors such as clinginess, jealousy, and a constant need for validation. These individuals may struggle with trust issues and fear being abandoned, which can lead to overly controlling or possessive behaviors. Their heightened sensitivity to any perceived signs of rejection can cause them to react emotionally, sometimes pushing their partners away in their attempts to hold onto them. This creates a self-fulfilling prophecy where their fear of abandonment becomes a reality due to their own actions.

Conversely, individuals with an avoidant attachment style tend to keep their partners at arm's length, avoiding emotional intimacy and commitment. They may appear emotionally distant, aloof, or uninterested in the relationship, which can be deeply frustrating for their partners. This detachment often stems from a fear of vulnerability and a belief that relying on others is a weakness. Avoidants may prioritize their independence and self-sufficiency to such an extent that they inadvertently push their partners away, leading to relationship breakdowns.

Both anxious and avoidant attachment styles can create significant challenges in relationships, particularly when paired with each other. The dynamic between an anxious and an avoidant partner can be particularly volatile, as one person's need for closeness clashes with the other's desire for distance. This push-pull dynamic can lead to a cycle of conflict, with each partner reinforcing the other's insecurities and attachment-related fears. Understanding these dynamics is crucial for breaking the cycle and creating a healthier, more balanced relationship.

Overview of Anxious and Avoidant Attachment

Anxious and avoidant attachment styles are two of the most common insecure attachment patterns that can significantly impact relationships. Individuals with an anxious attachment style often have a deep-seated fear of abandonment and a constant need for reassurance. This fear often stems from inconsistent caregiving in childhood, where the individual learned that love and attention were unpredictable and not always available. As a result, anxious individuals may become overly dependent on their partners, seeking constant affirmation of their worth and the stability of the relationship.

On the other hand, the avoidant attachment style is characterized by a strong desire for independence and self-reliance. Avoidant individuals often struggle with emotional intimacy and may keep their partners at a distance to protect themselves from potential rejection or hurt. This attachment style is typically developed in response to caregivers who were emotionally unavailable or dismissive of the child's needs. As a result, avoidant individuals learn to suppress their emotions and rely on themselves rather than others for support.

While both anxious and avoidant attachment styles can create challenges in relationships, they are not fixed or unchangeable. With self-awareness, effort, and the right tools, individuals can work towards developing a more secure attachment style, leading to healthier, more fulfilling relationships. It is important to recognize that these attachment patterns are not flaws or deficiencies but rather adaptive responses to early life experiences.

Understanding this can be a powerful motivator for change and healing.

The Path to Healing and Security

The journey from an insecure to a secure attachment style is a process that requires time, effort, and often professional support. Healing begins with self-awareness; recognizing one's attachment style and understanding how it influences thoughts, emotions, and behaviors in relationships. This awareness can be gained through self-reflection, journaling, therapy, or even reading about attachment theory. Once an individual has identified their attachment style, they can begin to take steps towards change.

For those with an anxious attachment style, healing involves learning to manage anxiety and reduce dependency on others for validation. This can be achieved through practices such as mindfulness, self-compassion, and developing a stronger sense of self-worth. Building trust in oneself and in others is also crucial, as is learning to communicate needs and desires in a healthy, assertive manner.

For those with an avoidant attachment style, the path to healing involves opening up to emotional vulnerability and learning to rely on others in a healthy way. This may require challenging deeply ingrained beliefs about independence and self-reliance, as well as developing greater empathy and emotional intimacy with others. Therapy can be particularly beneficial for avoidant individuals, as it provides a safe space to explore and express emotions.

Ultimately, the goal of healing is to develop a secure attachment style, characterized by balanced, healthy relationships where both partners feel safe, valued, and connected. This journey is not always easy, and setbacks are a normal part of the process. However, with persistence and support, individuals can move towards greater emotional balance and security, leading to more fulfilling and harmonious relationships.

Chapter 1

Understanding Attachment Styles

Attachment styles are fundamental to how individuals relate to others throughout their lives. They are deeply rooted in our earliest experiences and shape our behaviors, emotions, and perceptions in relationships. Understanding attachment styles is essential for anyone seeking to improve their relationships and emotional well-being. The concept of attachment styles comes from attachment theory, a psychological model that explains how the bonds formed in early childhood between a child and their caregiver impact their ability to form healthy relationships in adulthood. These attachment styles are not merely surface-level behaviors but are ingrained patterns that influence how we perceive ourselves, how we interact with others, and how we navigate the complexities of intimacy and connection. By delving into the origins of attachment theory and understanding the role of early childhood in shaping attachment styles, we can begin to uncover the roots of our relationship patterns and work towards more secure and fulfilling connections.

The Theory Behind Attachment Styles

Attachment theory is one of the most influential frameworks in psychology, particularly in understanding the development of personality and social behavior. It was initially developed by British psychiatrist and psychoanalyst John Bowlby in the mid-20th century. Bowlby was deeply interested in the bonds between children and their caregivers and how these early relationships influenced later behavior. His work was revolutionary in shifting the focus from innate drives and instincts, as proposed by Freudian theory, to the importance of early relationships and emotional bonds.

Bowlby's theory posits that the need for attachment is an evolutionary mechanism designed to ensure survival. In early human history, the attachment bond between a child and their caregiver was essential for the child's survival, providing protection, care, and support. This bond ensured that the child would remain close to the caregiver, increasing their chances of survival in a dangerous environment. Over time, these attachment behaviors became ingrained in human biology, shaping the way individuals seek and maintain relationships.

Bowlby identified that children are born with an innate system that motivates them to seek proximity to their primary caregiver, particularly when they are distressed or threatened. This system is known as the attachment behavioral system. The quality of the interactions between the child and the caregiver within this system plays a crucial role in shaping the child's attachment style. When a caregiver is consistently responsive and sensitive to a child's needs, the child is likely to develop a secure attachment style. Conversely, if the caregiver is inconsistent, unresponsive, or even neglectful, the child may develop an insecure attachment style, which can manifest as anxious, avoidant, or disorganized attachment in adulthood.

Mary Ainsworth, a colleague of Bowlby, expanded on his work by conducting a series of experiments known as the "Strange Situation" to observe the attachment behaviors of children in a controlled setting. Ainsworth's research provided empirical support for Bowlby's theories and led to the identification of different attachment styles: secure, anxious, avoidant, and later, disorganized. These styles describe the patterns of behavior that children exhibit when they are separated from and then reunited with their caregivers. Securely attached children show distress when their caregiver leaves but are quickly comforted upon their return. Anxiously attached children are overly distressed when separated and are difficult to soothe even when the caregiver returns. Avoidantly attached children show little distress upon separation and avoid the caregiver upon their return. Disorganized attachment, which was identified later by researchers, is characterized by a lack of a coherent strategy for dealing with separation and reunion, often reflecting a history of trauma or abuse.

Attachment theory has since been applied to adult relationships, where it has been used to explain how the attachment styles formed in childhood continue to influence our romantic relationships, friendships, and even relationships with colleagues and authority figures. The patterns of attachment we develop as children often carry over into adulthood, where they shape our expectations, behaviors, and emotional responses in relationships. Understanding these patterns can be incredibly empowering, allowing individuals to recognize and address unhealthy behaviors and work towards more secure and fulfilling relationships.

The Origins of Attachment Theory

The origins of attachment theory are rooted in Bowlby's early work with children who had been separated from their families during World War II. Bowlby observed that these children often exhibited behavioral problems and emotional difficulties, which he believed were linked to the disruption of their attachment bonds. His observations led him to hypothesize that the quality of the attachment bond between a child and their caregiver was crucial for the child's emotional and psychological development.

Bowlby's ideas were influenced by several disciplines, including psychoanalysis, ethology (the study of animal behavior), and cognitive psychology. He drew parallels between the attachment behaviors observed in children and the behaviors of animals in the wild, particularly in how young animals seek proximity to their mothers for protection. This interdisciplinary approach allowed Bowlby to develop a comprehensive theory that addressed both the biological and psychological aspects of attachment.

Bowlby's work was initially met with resistance from the psychoanalytic community, which was more focused on internal drives and unconscious conflicts. However, his theory gained widespread acceptance as more evidence emerged to support his ideas. The "Strange Situation" experiments conducted by Ainsworth provided critical empirical support for Bowlby's theory, demonstrating the different attachment styles and their impact on children's behavior. This research was groundbreaking in that it provided a clear framework for understanding the dynamics of attachment and how these dynamics play out in different contexts.

Over time, attachment theory has been expanded and refined by researchers and clinicians. The concept of attachment styles has been applied to various aspects of human behavior, including romantic relationships, parenting, and even workplace dynamics. It has also been used to develop therapeutic approaches aimed at helping individuals understand and heal from attachment-related issues. For example, attachment-based therapy focuses on helping individuals develop a more secure attachment style by addressing the underlying fears and anxieties that contribute to insecure attachment behaviors.

Attachment theory has also been influential in the field of developmental psychology, where it has been used to understand the long-term impact of early childhood experiences on emotional and psychological development. Research has shown that individuals with secure attachment styles tend to have better mental health outcomes, including higher self-esteem, better stress management, and more satisfying relationships. Conversely, those with insecure attachment styles are more likely to experience mental health challenges, such as anxiety, depression, and difficulties in forming and maintaining healthy relationships.

The Role of Early Childhood in Shaping Attachment Styles

Early childhood is a critical period for the development of attachment styles, as this is when the foundational attachment bonds are formed. The interactions between a child and their primary caregiver during this period play a significant role in shaping the child's attachment style. The consistency, responsiveness, and sensitivity of the caregiver are key factors in determining whether the child will develop a secure or insecure attachment style.

A secure attachment style typically develops when the caregiver is consistently responsive to the child's needs. This means that when the child is hungry, scared, or in need of comfort, the caregiver is there to provide the necessary support. Over time, the child learns to trust that their caregiver will be there for them, which fosters a sense of security and confidence in their relationships. This secure base allows the child to explore their environment, knowing that they can return to their caregiver for comfort and support when needed. As a result, securely attached children tend to be more resilient, confident, and capable of forming healthy relationships later in life.

In contrast, an anxious attachment style may develop when the caregiver is inconsistent in their responsiveness. For example, a caregiver who is sometimes attentive and caring but at other times neglectful or emotionally unavailable can create a sense of unpredictability for the child. The child may become anxious about whether their needs will be met, leading them to become clingy, overly dependent, or constantly seeking reassurance in their relationships. This anxiety can carry over into adulthood, where it manifests as a fear of abandonment and a tendency to become overly attached to others.

An avoidant attachment style may develop when the caregiver is consistently unresponsive or dismissive of the child's needs. In this scenario, the child learns that expressing their needs or seeking comfort will not result in the desired response from the caregiver. As a result, the child may suppress their emotions and become overly self-reliant, avoiding emotional intimacy and close relationships. In adulthood, this can lead to difficulties in forming deep emotional connections and a tendency to keep others at a distance.

Disorganized attachment, which is often associated with trauma or abuse, can develop when the caregiver is a source of both comfort and fear. In such cases, the child may experience confusion and conflict, as they are drawn to the caregiver for safety but also fearful of them due to past experiences of harm or neglect. This disorganized attachment style can lead to significant challenges in forming stable and healthy relationships in adulthood, as the individual may struggle with trust, emotional regulation, and consistent behavior in relationships.

The role of early childhood in shaping attachment styles highlights the importance of nurturing and responsive caregiving in promoting healthy emotional and psychological development. While the attachment styles formed in childhood can have a lasting impact on relationships, it is important to note that they are not fixed. With self-awareness, therapy, and intentional effort, individuals can work towards developing a more secure attachment style, leading to more fulfilling and balanced relationships in adulthood. Understanding the origins and development of attachment styles is the first step in this journey towards healing and emotional growth.

Identifying Anxious and Avoidant Attachment

Understanding the key characteristics of anxious and avoidant attachment styles is essential for recognizing these patterns in oneself and others. These attachment styles manifest in distinct behaviors and emotional responses that can significantly impact the quality and dynamics of relationships. Identifying these characteristics allows individuals to gain insight into their relational patterns and provides a foundation for personal growth and healing.

Key Characteristics of Anxious Attachment

Anxious attachment is characterized by a deep-seated fear of abandonment and a strong desire for closeness and reassurance in relationships. Individuals with this attachment style often experience intense anxiety about the stability of their relationships and may feel an overwhelming need for validation and attention from their partners. This neediness can lead to behaviors that are perceived as clingy or overly dependent.

One of the most prominent characteristics of anxious attachment is hypervigilance regarding any signs of potential rejection or abandonment. Anxiously attached individuals are highly sensitive to changes in their partner's behavior, tone, or mood, often interpreting minor fluctuations as indications of impending rejection. This heightened sensitivity can lead to excessive worry and preoccupation with the relationship, resulting in frequent attempts to seek reassurance from the partner.

In addition to this hypervigilance, individuals with anxious attachment may also struggle with self-esteem issues. They may have a negative self-image and feel unworthy of love or attention, which can exacerbate their fears of abandonment. This low self-esteem often leads to a pattern of seeking constant validation from their partner, as they rely on external affirmation to feel secure and valued.

Anxiously attached individuals may also engage in behaviors aimed at keeping their partner close, such as excessive communication, attempts to control the relationship, or even manipulative tactics. These behaviors are often driven by a fear of losing the partner and are intended to maintain the closeness and security that the individual desperately seeks. However, these actions can sometimes have the opposite effect, pushing the partner away and reinforcing the individual's fears of abandonment.

Key Characteristics of Avoidant Attachment

Avoidant attachment is characterized by a strong emphasis on independence and self-reliance, often at the expense of emotional intimacy and closeness in relationships. Individuals with this attachment style tend to prioritize their autonomy and may feel uncomfortable with too much emotional closeness or dependence on others. As a result, they may distance themselves emotionally from their partners, avoiding vulnerability and intimacy.

One of the key characteristics of avoidant attachment is a tendency to suppress or downplay emotions. Avoidantly attached individuals often struggle to express their feelings or may appear emotionally detached or indifferent. This detachment is often a defense mechanism, developed to protect themselves from potential hurt or rejection. By keeping their emotions at bay, avoidantly attached individuals maintain a sense of control and protect themselves from the perceived risks of emotional intimacy.

Another characteristic of avoidant attachment is a reluctance to commit to relationships or fully engage in them. Avoidantly attached individuals may fear becoming too dependent on others or losing their independence, leading them to keep their partners at a distance. They may avoid discussing the future of the relationship or may downplay the significance of the relationship altogether. This reluctance to commit can create tension and frustration for their partners, who may feel that the avoidantly attached individual is not fully invested in the relationship.

Avoidantly attached individuals may also have a negative view of others, often seeing them as overly needy or demanding. This perspective can lead to a dismissive or critical attitude towards their partner's emotional needs, further contributing to emotional distance in the relationship. Despite their outward appearance of self-sufficiency, avoidantly attached individuals may struggle with feelings of loneliness or emptiness, as their avoidance of emotional closeness prevents them from forming deep, meaningful connections.

How These Styles Manifest in Adult Relationships

In adult relationships, anxious and avoidant attachment styles can create a dynamic that is often referred to as the "anxious-avoidant trap." This dynamic occurs when an anxiously attached individual pairs with an avoidantly attached partner. The anxious partner's need for closeness and reassurance clashes with the avoidant partner's need for distance and independence, creating a push-pull pattern that can be highly distressing for both parties.

In this dynamic, the anxious partner may constantly seek reassurance and closeness, while the avoidant partner may withdraw in response to this perceived pressure. The more the anxious partner pushes for closeness, the more the avoidant partner pulls away, leading to a cycle of conflict and emotional distress. This pattern can be challenging to break, as each partner's behavior reinforces the other's attachment-related fears and insecurities.

For anxiously attached individuals, relationships can be a source of significant anxiety and emotional turmoil. They may find themselves constantly worrying about the stability of the relationship, fearing that their partner will leave them or stop loving them. This anxiety can lead to behaviors that are intended to secure the relationship, such as excessive communication, jealousy, or attempts to control the partner's behavior. However, these actions can sometimes have the opposite effect, pushing the partner away and exacerbating the individual's fears of abandonment.

For avoidantly attached individuals, relationships can feel suffocating or overwhelming. They may struggle to balance their desire for independence with their partner's need for closeness, leading to a pattern of emotional withdrawal or avoidance. Avoidantly attached individuals may prioritize their personal space and autonomy over the relationship, leading to feelings of loneliness or dissatisfaction for both partners. Despite their desire for independence, avoidantly attached individuals may also experience feelings of insecurity or fear of rejection, which they may mask with emotional detachment.

The Secure Attachment: What It Looks Like

A secure attachment style is the ideal attachment pattern, characterized by a healthy balance of intimacy, autonomy, and emotional regulation. Securely attached individuals have a positive view of themselves and others, allowing them to form stable, trusting, and fulfilling relationships. Unlike their anxiously or avoidantly attached counterparts, securely attached individuals are comfortable with both closeness and independence, and they are able to navigate the complexities of relationships with confidence and emotional resilience.

Traits of Secure Attachment

Securely attached individuals exhibit a range of traits that contribute to the stability and health of their relationships. One of the most notable traits is emotional regulation. Securely attached individuals are able to manage their emotions effectively, even in stressful or challenging situations. They are not easily overwhelmed by anxiety or fear and are able to approach relationship issues with a calm and rational mindset. This emotional stability allows them to communicate their needs and feelings openly and constructively, fostering a positive and supportive relational environment.

Another key trait of secure attachment is the ability to form deep, meaningful connections with others. Securely attached individuals are comfortable with emotional intimacy and are able to trust their partners without fear of abandonment or betrayal. This trust is based on a positive view of both themselves and others, allowing them to give and receive love freely. They are also capable of being independent without feeling threatened by their partner's need for closeness, creating a balanced and harmonious relationship dynamic.

Securely attached individuals are also effective communicators. They are able to express their needs, desires, and boundaries clearly and respectfully, and they are equally receptive to their partner's needs and feelings. This open and honest communication fosters mutual understanding and respect, allowing both partners to feel valued and supported in the relationship. Securely attached individuals are also empathetic and compassionate, able to understand and respond to their partner's emotions in a caring and supportive manner.

The Benefits of a Secure Attachment Style

The benefits of a secure attachment style are numerous and far-reaching, impacting not only romantic relationships but also friendships, family dynamics, and even professional relationships. One of the primary benefits is the ability to form and maintain stable, long-lasting relationships. Securely attached individuals are able to build trust and intimacy with their partners, leading to relationships that are both emotionally fulfilling and resilient in the face of challenges.

Secure attachment also promotes a sense of self-confidence and emotional well-being. Securely attached individuals have a positive self-image and are able to approach relationships from a place of strength and security. They are not overly dependent on their partners for validation or self-worth, allowing them to maintain a healthy sense of independence within the relationship. This self-confidence also translates into a greater ability to handle conflict and adversity, as securely attached individuals are able to approach problems with a calm and constructive mindset.

In addition to these personal benefits, secure attachment also contributes to the overall health and stability of the relationship. Securely attached individuals are more likely to engage in positive relationship behaviors, such as effective communication, empathy, and emotional support. These behaviors create a positive feedback loop, where both partners feel valued and supported, leading to greater relationship satisfaction and longevity.

How to Identify Securely Attached Individuals

Identifying securely attached individuals involves observing their behaviors, attitudes, and emotional responses in relationships. Securely attached individuals are typically calm and confident in their interactions with others. They are comfortable with both giving and receiving affection, and they are able to express their emotions openly and honestly. In relationships, they are supportive and responsive to their partner's needs, while also maintaining their own independence and self-worth.

Securely attached individuals are also effective problem-solvers. They approach conflicts with a collaborative mindset, seeking to find solutions that are mutually beneficial. They are not easily threatened by differences or disagreements and are able to navigate relationship challenges with a sense of calm and rationality. Their ability to manage conflict constructively is a key indicator of secure attachment, as it reflects their emotional stability and resilience.

In addition to these traits, securely attached individuals are also likely to have a strong support network of friends and family. They value their relationships with others and are able to maintain healthy, balanced connections in all areas of their life. This ability to form and maintain positive relationships is a hallmark of secure attachment and is indicative of a well-developed sense of emotional intelligence and interpersonal skills.

By understanding and identifying these traits, individuals can recognize secure attachment in themselves and others, fostering healthier and more fulfilling relationships. For those who do not yet have a secure attachment style, identifying these traits can also provide a roadmap for personal growth and development

Chapter 2

The Roots of Anxious and Avoidant Attachment

Childhood Influences and Family Dynamics

The roots of anxious and avoidant attachment styles are deeply embedded in early childhood experiences, particularly in the interactions between a child and their primary caregivers. These early experiences play a crucial role in shaping an individual's attachment style, which in turn influences their emotional and relational patterns throughout life. Understanding the impact of childhood influences and family dynamics is essential for comprehending how these attachment styles develop and manifest in adulthood.

The foundation of attachment theory, originally proposed by John Bowlby, emphasizes the importance of the bond between a child and their caregiver. According to Bowlby, a child's sense of security is largely determined by the responsiveness and availability of their caregiver.

When caregivers consistently meet a child's needs for comfort, protection, and emotional support, the child is likely to develop a secure attachment. However, when these needs are inconsistently met or neglected, the child may develop an insecure attachment, which can take the form of either anxious or avoidant attachment.

The Impact of Parenting Styles

Parenting styles play a significant role in the formation of attachment styles. The way in which a caregiver responds to a child's emotional and physical needs can have a lasting impact on the child's sense of security and their ability to form healthy relationships in the future. There are various parenting styles that can influence the development of anxious or avoidant attachment, each with its own set of characteristics and outcomes.

In cases where caregivers are overly protective or excessively involved in the child's life, the child may develop an anxious attachment style. These caregivers may be quick to respond to the child's needs but may also exhibit behaviors that are intrusive or controlling. This over-involvement can prevent the child from developing a sense of autonomy and self-efficacy, leading to a heightened dependence on the caregiver for validation and support. As a result, the child may grow up with an intense fear of abandonment and a constant need for reassurance in their relationships. The anxiously attached individual may become preoccupied with their relationships, constantly seeking signs of approval and fearing rejection or separation.

Conversely, avoidant attachment often develops in response to caregiving that is emotionally distant or neglectful. Caregivers who are unresponsive to the child's emotional needs, or who discourage the expression of emotions, may inadvertently teach the child that their feelings are unimportant or unwelcome. In such environments, the child learns to suppress their emotions and becomes self-reliant, as a way to protect themselves from the pain of unmet needs. This self-reliance and emotional suppression can lead to the development of an avoidant attachment style, characterized by a preference for independence and discomfort with emotional intimacy. Avoidantly attached individuals may struggle to express their feelings or connect deeply with others, often keeping their partners at an emotional distance.

It is important to note that parenting styles are often influenced by a variety of factors, including the parents' own attachment histories, cultural norms, and external stressors such as financial difficulties or health issues. These factors can contribute to the complexity of the parent-child relationship and the subsequent development of attachment styles. For example, a parent who was raised in an emotionally distant household may struggle to provide the emotional warmth and support that their child needs, perpetuating a cycle of avoidant attachment across generations. Similarly, a parent who is overwhelmed by external stressors may be less attuned to their child's emotional needs, leading to inconsistencies in caregiving and the potential development of an anxious attachment style.

Family Environment and Emotional Development

The broader family environment also plays a critical role in the development of attachment styles. A child's emotional development is influenced not only by their relationship with their primary caregiver but also by the overall emotional climate of the family. Factors such as the presence of conflict, the availability of emotional support, and the modeling of healthy relational behaviors all contribute to the child's understanding of relationships and their own emotional regulation.

In families where there is a high level of conflict, children may be exposed to negative relational patterns that can impact their attachment style. For example, a child who witnesses frequent arguments or emotional outbursts may internalize these behaviors as normal or expected in relationships. This exposure can lead to difficulties in managing their own emotions and navigating interpersonal conflicts. In some cases, the child may develop an anxious attachment style, becoming hypervigilant to signs of conflict and overly focused on maintaining harmony in their relationships. Alternatively, they may develop an avoidant attachment style, distancing themselves emotionally as a way to avoid the discomfort of conflict.

On the other hand, a family environment that provides emotional support and models healthy relational behaviors can foster the development of a secure attachment style. In such environments, children learn to trust that their emotional needs will be met and that relationships can be a source of comfort and security. They are encouraged to express their feelings openly and are provided with the tools to manage their emotions effectively. This foundation of emotional security allows them to develop a positive view of themselves and others, leading to healthier and more fulfilling relationships in adulthood.

The presence of siblings and extended family members can also influence a child's attachment style. Sibling relationships, in particular, can serve as a model for peer relationships and can impact the child's social and emotional development. In families where there is a strong sense of support and cohesion among siblings, children may develop a secure attachment style, characterized by a positive view of relationships and a willingness to engage in emotional intimacy. Conversely, in families where sibling relationships are marked by rivalry or emotional distance, children may be more likely to develop insecure attachment styles, either anxious or avoidant.

In addition to the immediate family environment, cultural and societal factors also play a role in shaping attachment styles. Cultural norms and expectations regarding parenting, emotional expression, and independence can influence how attachment styles are formed and how they manifest in relationships. For example, in cultures that value independence and self-reliance, there may be a greater prevalence of avoidant attachment styles, as children are encouraged to be emotionally self-sufficient from a young age. Conversely, in cultures that emphasize close family bonds and interdependence, there may be a higher prevalence of anxious attachment styles, as children are raised to prioritize relational closeness and emotional connection.

The roots of anxious and avoidant attachment styles are deeply intertwined with childhood influences and family dynamics. Parenting styles, family environment, and broader cultural factors all contribute to the development of these attachment patterns, which can have lasting effects on an individual's emotional and relational well-being. Understanding these roots is essential for recognizing the origins of one's attachment style and for embarking on a path toward healing and secure attachment. By exploring the impact of early experiences on attachment, individuals can gain valuable insights into their relational patterns and take steps toward developing healthier, more secure relationships.

Trauma and Its Effects on Attachment

Trauma, particularly in childhood, can have profound and lasting effects on the development of attachment styles. When children experience traumatic events, such as abuse, neglect, or significant loss, the way they relate to others can be deeply altered. Trauma can disrupt the natural development of secure attachment, leading to the creation or reinforcement of insecure attachment styles such as anxious or avoidant attachment. The emotional scars left by trauma can make it difficult for individuals to trust others, feel safe in relationships, or believe in their own worthiness of love and connection.

How Trauma Can Create or Reinforce Insecure Attachments

Trauma often distorts a child's perception of the world and their place in it, particularly in relation to their caregivers. For example, a child who experiences abuse or neglect from a primary caregiver; the very person meant to provide safety and love, may develop a worldview in which relationships are inherently unsafe. This belief can lead to the formation of an avoidant attachment style, where the child learns to distance themselves emotionally to avoid further pain. As they grow older, avoidantly attached individuals may struggle to form deep connections with others, fearing vulnerability and intimacy because of their early experiences.

In other cases, trauma can lead to the development of an anxious attachment style. A child who experiences inconsistent caregiving, where love and attention are given unpredictably, may become hyper-focused on seeking approval and validation from their caregivers. This pattern can extend into adulthood, with the anxiously attached individual constantly fearing abandonment and desperately seeking reassurance in their relationships. The trauma of unpredictability in their early years makes them highly sensitive to any perceived threats to their relationships, leading to behaviors that are often rooted in fear and insecurity.

Trauma can also reinforce existing insecure attachment patterns. For instance, a child who already exhibits signs of anxious attachment may become even more anxious if they experience trauma such as parental divorce or the sudden loss of a loved one. Similarly, a child with avoidant tendencies may further retreat into emotional withdrawal if they are exposed to traumatic experiences that reinforce their belief that emotional closeness leads to pain. These reinforced patterns can become deeply ingrained, making it challenging to develop healthier, more secure attachment styles later in life.

The effects of trauma on attachment are not limited to the immediate aftermath of the traumatic event. Often, the impact of trauma lingers into adulthood, influencing how individuals relate to others, perceive themselves, and navigate the complexities of relationships. The fear, mistrust, and emotional turmoil stemming from early trauma can create significant barriers to forming secure attachments, making it difficult for individuals to experience the stability, trust, and intimacy that characterize healthy relationships.

Overcoming Childhood Trauma to Heal Attachment Wounds

Healing from childhood trauma and its effects on attachment is a complex and often lengthy process, but it is possible with the right support and strategies. The journey toward healing begins with recognizing and acknowledging the impact of trauma on one's attachment style. Understanding how past experiences have shaped current relational patterns is a critical first step in breaking the cycle of insecure attachment.

Therapeutic interventions, particularly those that focus on trauma, can be instrumental in helping individuals heal from attachment-related wounds. Approaches such as trauma-focused cognitive-behavioral therapy (TF-CBT), eye movement desensitization and reprocessing (EMDR), and attachment-based therapy can provide individuals with the tools they need to process their trauma and develop healthier attachment patterns. These therapies often involve revisiting and reprocessing traumatic memories in a safe and supportive environment, allowing individuals to integrate these experiences and reduce their emotional charge.

Building new, positive relational experiences is another key component of healing attachment wounds. Forming relationships with individuals who are consistently supportive, trustworthy, and emotionally available can help rewire the brain's attachment system. Over time, these positive experiences can replace the negative associations formed by early trauma, allowing individuals to develop a more secure attachment style. Trust and intimacy, which may have been damaged by trauma, can be rebuilt through relationships that provide a safe space for vulnerability and emotional connection.

Self-awareness and self-compassion are also crucial in the healing process. Individuals who have experienced trauma must learn to recognize their attachment-related triggers and patterns and develop strategies to manage them. This might include practicing mindfulness, setting healthy boundaries, and engaging in self-care activities that promote emotional well-being. By cultivating a compassionate understanding of their own experiences, individuals can begin to heal the wounds of the past and move toward more secure and fulfilling relationships.

The Role of Social and Cultural Factors

Attachment styles are not developed in a vacuum; they are influenced by a variety of social and cultural factors that shape how individuals perceive and engage in relationships. These factors play a significant role in the formation and expression of attachment styles, both in childhood and throughout adulthood. Understanding the role of social and cultural influences is essential for a comprehensive view of attachment and how it manifests across different contexts.

Cultural Influences on Attachment Styles

Cultural norms and values deeply influence the development and expression of attachment styles. Different cultures have varying expectations regarding family roles, emotional expression, and independence, all of which can impact how attachment styles are formed and maintained. For example, in collectivist cultures, where the emphasis is on interdependence and close family ties, there may be a greater tendency toward anxious attachment. In these cultures, individuals are often raised with the expectation that family and community relationships are central to one's identity and well-being, which can lead to a heightened sensitivity to relational disruptions and a stronger need for reassurance and closeness.

Conversely, in individualistic cultures, where independence and self-reliance are highly valued, there may be a greater prevalence of avoidant attachment. In such environments, children may be encouraged to develop autonomy from an early age, leading to a preference for emotional distance and self-sufficiency in relationships. These cultural norms can shape how attachment is expressed and understood, influencing everything from parenting styles to expectations in romantic partnerships.

Cultural influences also extend to gender roles and expectations, which can impact how attachment styles are expressed differently by men and women. In some cultures, traditional gender roles may discourage men from expressing vulnerability or emotional dependence, potentially reinforcing avoidant attachment patterns. Women, on the other hand, may be socialized to prioritize relationships and caregiving, which could reinforce anxious attachment behaviors. These gendered expectations can complicate the expression of attachment styles, leading to differences in how men and women experience and navigate relationships.

Socialization and Peer Relationships

Socialization; the process by which individuals learn and internalize the values, norms, and behaviors of their society, also plays a crucial role in shaping attachment styles. From a young age, children learn about relationships through their interactions with peers, teachers, and other social figures. These early social experiences can reinforce or challenge the attachment patterns formed within the family.

Peer relationships, in particular, are significant in the development of attachment styles. Friendships provide children with opportunities to practice social skills, develop empathy, and learn about trust and reciprocity. Positive peer relationships can help children develop a secure attachment style, as they learn that relationships can be a source of support and joy. However, negative experiences with peers, such as bullying or social rejection, can reinforce insecure attachment patterns. An anxiously attached child, for example, may become even more fearful of rejection after experiencing social exclusion, while an avoidantly attached child may withdraw further from social interactions.

As individuals grow older, their social networks expand, and the influence of peer relationships continues to play a significant role in shaping attachment styles. Romantic relationships, in particular, can either reinforce existing attachment patterns or provide opportunities for growth and change. For instance, an individual with an anxious attachment style may find that a relationship with a securely attached partner helps them develop greater emotional stability and security. Conversely, a relationship with an avoidantly attached partner may reinforce their fears of abandonment and perpetuate the cycle of anxiety.

Socialization also includes the broader societal messages conveyed through media, education, and community norms. These messages can influence how individuals view relationships and attachment. For example, media portrayals of romance often idealize certain attachment behaviors, such as the intense pursuit of a partner (which may align with anxious attachment) or the stoic, independent hero (which may align with avoidant attachment). These portrayals can shape individuals' expectations and behaviors in their own relationships, sometimes reinforcing insecure attachment patterns.

In summary, social and cultural factors play a significant role in the development and expression of attachment styles. Cultural norms, gender expectations, and socialization processes all contribute to how individuals form, maintain, and understand relationships. By recognizing the influence of these factors, individuals can gain a deeper understanding of their own attachment patterns and how they may be shaped by the broader social context. This awareness is a crucial step in the journey toward developing healthier, more secure attachment styles and fostering more fulfilling relationships.

Chapter 3

Healing Anxious Attachment

Recognizing Anxious Attachment in Yourself

Healing anxious attachment begins with recognizing its presence within yourself. Anxious attachment is often characterized by a deep fear of abandonment, a constant need for reassurance, and an overwhelming preoccupation with relationships. Individuals with this attachment style may find themselves constantly worrying about their partner's feelings, doubting their own worth, and fearing that they will be left behind. This anxiety can be all-consuming, leading to behaviors that can strain relationships, such as clinginess, excessive communication, or difficulty trusting others.

To begin the healing process, self-reflection is crucial. This involves taking a step back and honestly assessing your patterns in relationships. Reflect on past and present relationships, noting any recurring themes of insecurity, jealousy, or fear of being alone. Ask yourself if you often feel anxious when your partner is not immediately responsive or if you find yourself needing constant validation from them. These reflections can provide insight into the underlying fears and beliefs driving your anxious attachment.

Self-reflection exercises can be particularly helpful in recognizing anxious attachment. Journaling is one such exercise, where you can document your thoughts, feelings, and reactions in your relationships. Writing down your experiences allows you to identify patterns and triggers that may not be immediately obvious. For example, you may notice that your anxiety spikes when your partner is busy with other commitments, leading you to feel neglected or unimportant. By identifying these triggers, you can begin to understand the root causes of your anxious attachment and work towards addressing them.

Another useful exercise is to engage in mindfulness meditation. Mindfulness involves paying attention to your thoughts and feelings in the present moment without judgment. This practice can help you become more aware of the anxious thoughts that arise in your mind, allowing you to observe them without getting swept away by them. Over time, mindfulness can help you develop a more balanced perspective on your relationships, reducing the intensity of your anxiety and helping you respond to situations more calmly and thoughtfully.

Recognizing anxious attachment also involves understanding the impact it has on your relationships. Reflect on how your anxiety influences your behavior towards your partner. Do you find yourself seeking constant reassurance, even when there is no real threat to the relationship? Do you become overly sensitive to perceived signs of disinterest or rejection? Understanding these behaviors is essential for taking responsibility for your part in the relationship dynamics and for beginning the work of healing.

Identifying triggers and patterns is another critical step in recognizing anxious attachment. Triggers are specific situations or behaviors that cause your anxiety to spike, such as when your partner doesn't respond to your messages right away or when they spend time with friends without you. By identifying these triggers, you can begin to anticipate when your anxiety is likely to arise and take steps to manage it before it becomes overwhelming. Patterns, on the other hand, are the habitual ways you respond to these triggers. For example, you may notice that whenever you feel anxious, you immediately reach out to your partner for reassurance, even if it's not necessary. Recognizing these patterns allows you to interrupt them and choose healthier responses.

Strategies for Building Security

Once you've recognized the presence of anxious attachment in yourself, the next step is to develop strategies for building a sense of security in your relationships. This involves learning techniques to manage your anxiety, developing self-awareness and emotional regulation, and setting healthy boundaries that protect both your emotional well-being and the health of your relationships.

One of the most effective strategies for managing anxiety in relationships is to practice self-soothing techniques. These are methods that help you calm yourself when you start to feel anxious or insecure. Deep breathing exercises, for example, can help slow down your heart rate and reduce the physical symptoms of anxiety. When you feel your anxiety rising, take a few deep breaths, focusing on the sensation of the air entering and leaving your body. This simple practice can help ground you in the present moment and prevent your anxiety from spiraling out of control.

Another technique for managing anxiety is to challenge the negative thoughts that often accompany anxious attachment. These thoughts might include beliefs such as "I'm not good enough," "They're going to leave me," or "I always ruin relationships." It's important to recognize that these thoughts are not necessarily based on reality; rather, they are a reflection of your fears and insecurities. When these thoughts arise, try to counter them with more balanced and rational perspectives. For example, if you find yourself thinking, "They don't care about me because they didn't text back right away," challenge this by considering alternative explanations, such as they might be busy or preoccupied. By reframing your thoughts in a more positive light, you can reduce the intensity of your anxiety and maintain a healthier outlook on your relationship.

Developing self-awareness and emotional regulation is also crucial in healing anxious attachment. Self-awareness involves understanding your own emotions, needs, and triggers, while emotional regulation refers to your ability to manage your emotions in a healthy way. One way to develop these skills is through therapy, particularly cognitive-behavioral therapy (CBT), which can help you identify and change the thought patterns that contribute to your anxiety. Therapy can also provide you with tools to regulate your emotions, such as practicing relaxation techniques or learning how to communicate your needs more effectively in your relationships.

In addition to therapy, practicing self-compassion can be a powerful tool for emotional regulation. Self-compassion involves treating yourself with the same kindness and understanding that you would offer a close friend. When you start to feel anxious or insecure, instead of criticizing yourself or feeling ashamed, try to offer yourself reassurance and comfort. Remind yourself that it's okay to feel vulnerable and that your feelings are valid. By cultivating self-compassion, you can create a more nurturing inner environment, which can help reduce the intensity of your anxious attachment.

Setting healthy boundaries is another essential strategy for building security in your relationships. Boundaries are the limits you set with others to protect your emotional well-being. For individuals with anxious attachment, setting boundaries can be challenging, as there may be a fear that doing so will push others away. However, boundaries are necessary for maintaining a sense of autonomy and self-respect in relationships. Start by identifying your own needs and limits; what behaviors or situations make you feel uncomfortable or unsafe? Once you have a clear understanding of your boundaries, communicate them openly and assertively to your partner. This might involve expressing your need for space when you're feeling overwhelmed or setting limits on how much reassurance you seek from your partner. Healthy boundaries help create a more balanced relationship dynamic, where both partners feel respected and valued.

Building security in your relationships also involves developing a stronger sense of self-worth. Individuals with anxious attachment often struggle with feelings of inadequacy or unworthiness, which can fuel their anxiety in relationships. Working on building your self-esteem can help you feel more secure and confident in your relationships. This might involve setting personal goals, pursuing activities that bring you joy, or surrounding yourself with supportive and affirming people. By cultivating a stronger sense of self-worth, you can reduce your dependence on external validation and feel more secure in your relationships.

Healing anxious attachment requires a combination of self-reflection, self-awareness, and practical strategies for managing anxiety and building security. Recognizing anxious attachment within yourself is the first step, followed by developing techniques to manage your anxiety, such as self-soothing and challenging negative thoughts. Developing self-awareness and emotional regulation, as well as setting healthy boundaries, are also crucial components of the healing process. By taking these steps, you can begin to break free from the cycle of anxious attachment and move toward more secure, fulfilling relationships.

Strengthening Communication in Relationships

Effective communication is the cornerstone of any healthy relationship, and this is especially true for individuals working to heal anxious attachment. When communication is clear, honest, and compassionate, it creates a safe space where both partners can express their needs and concerns without fear of judgment or rejection. Strengthening communication skills can help you express your needs more effectively, build trust in your relationship, and reduce dependency, ultimately fostering a more secure attachment.

How to Express Needs Without Fear

One of the biggest challenges for individuals with anxious attachment is expressing their needs without fear of being dismissed or rejected. This fear often stems from past experiences where their needs may have been neglected or met with criticism, leading to a deep-seated belief that their desires are burdensome or unwelcome. However, learning to communicate your needs clearly and confidently is essential for building healthier relationships.

The first step in expressing your needs without fear is to recognize and validate those needs within yourself. Understand that your needs are legitimate and deserving of attention, regardless of how others may have responded to them in the past. By acknowledging the importance of your needs, you can approach communication with greater self-assurance and clarity.

When communicating your needs, it's important to use "I" statements, which focus on your own feelings and experiences rather than placing blame on your partner. For example, instead of saying, "You never spend time with me," you might say, "I feel lonely when we don't spend quality time together." This approach helps to prevent your partner from becoming defensive and encourages a more open and constructive dialogue.

It's also helpful to be specific and direct when expressing your needs. Avoid vague statements that can be easily misinterpreted. Instead, clearly articulate what you need and why it's important to you. For instance, instead of saying, "I need more attention," you could say, "I would feel more connected if we could set aside some time each week to have a meaningful conversation." Specific requests make it easier for your partner to understand and respond to your needs.

Expressing your needs without fear also involves managing your expectations. Understand that your partner may not always be able to meet your needs exactly as you envision, and that's okay. Healthy communication involves negotiation and compromise, where both partners work together to find a solution that honors each other's needs and boundaries. By approaching communication with a mindset of collaboration rather than demand, you can reduce the anxiety associated with expressing your needs and foster a more supportive and understanding relationship.

Building Trust and Reducing Dependency

Building trust is a fundamental aspect of healing anxious attachment and creating a more secure bond with your partner. Trust is built through consistent, positive experiences over time, where both partners demonstrate reliability, honesty, and respect for each other's feelings and boundaries. For individuals with anxious attachment, building trust often involves overcoming past hurts and learning to believe in the stability and resilience of their relationships.

One way to build trust is to focus on your own emotional independence. While it's natural to seek support and reassurance from your partner, it's also important to develop a strong sense of self-reliance. This doesn't mean shutting your partner out; rather, it means cultivating the ability to soothe and validate yourself, so that you're not entirely dependent on your partner for emotional stability.

Engaging in self-care practices, pursuing personal interests, and maintaining a support network outside of your relationship can all contribute to a greater sense of independence.

Another key to building trust is to consistently communicate with honesty and transparency. This includes being open about your feelings, even when they're difficult to share, and being willing to listen to your partner's concerns without judgment. Trust grows when both partners feel that they can share their true selves without fear of criticism or abandonment. Additionally, it's important to follow through on your commitments and promises, as reliability is a cornerstone of trust.

Reducing dependency in a relationship involves balancing your emotional needs with your partner's autonomy. It's natural to want closeness and connection, but it's also important to respect your partner's need for space and individuality. This balance can be achieved by setting healthy boundaries, where both partners agree on the amount of time and attention they can realistically give to each other. By respecting each other's boundaries and acknowledging that a healthy relationship includes both togetherness and individuality, you can create a more balanced and secure dynamic.

Building trust and reducing dependency also requires patience and persistence. Trust is not built overnight, and it may take time to fully heal from past attachment wounds. However, by consistently practicing open communication, emotional independence, and mutual respect, you can gradually build a stronger foundation of trust in your relationship.

Effective Conflict Resolution Skills

Conflict is a natural part of any relationship, but for individuals with anxious attachment, it can be particularly distressing. The fear of conflict escalating into rejection or abandonment can cause anxious individuals to either avoid confrontation altogether or react with intense emotion, both of which can strain the relationship. Developing effective conflict resolution skills is essential for managing disagreements in a healthy way and preventing them from undermining the security of your relationship.

One of the most important aspects of conflict resolution is learning to stay calm and composed during disagreements. This can be challenging for those with anxious attachment, as conflict often triggers deep-seated fears and insecurities. To manage these emotions, it can be helpful to practice deep breathing, mindfulness, or other calming techniques before engaging in a difficult conversation. By approaching conflict with a calm and measured demeanor, you're more likely to think clearly and communicate effectively.

Effective conflict resolution also involves active listening. This means fully focusing on what your partner is saying, without interrupting or planning your response while they're speaking. Active listening demonstrates respect and empathy, showing your partner that you value their perspective. It also helps you to better understand their point of view, which is crucial for finding a resolution that satisfies both parties.

When discussing a conflict, it's important to focus on the issue at hand rather than bringing up past grievances. Stick to the current situation and avoid generalizing ("You always" or "You never" statements) as these can escalate the conflict and make resolution more difficult. Instead, address specific behaviors or events and how they made you feel. This keeps the conversation focused and constructive.

Compromise is another key component of effective conflict resolution. In any disagreement, it's unlikely that one partner will get exactly what they want. Instead, aim for a solution that meets both of your needs to some extent. This might involve both partners making concessions or finding a middle ground. Compromise requires flexibility and a willingness to prioritize the relationship over winning the argument.

Finally, it's essential to repair the relationship after a conflict has been resolved. This might involve expressing appreciation for your partner's willingness to work through the disagreement or reaffirming your commitment to the relationship. Post-conflict repair helps to restore emotional closeness and ensures that both partners feel valued and understood.

In summary, strengthening communication in relationships is a multifaceted process that involves expressing needs without fear, building trust, reducing dependency, and developing effective conflict resolution skills. By working on these areas, individuals with anxious attachment can foster more secure, fulfilling, and resilient relationships. Through clear communication, mutual respect, and a commitment to growth, you can create a relationship environment where both partners feel safe, valued, and connected.

Chapter 4

Overcoming Avoidant Attachment

Identifying Avoidant Patterns in Your Life

Overcoming avoidant attachment begins with the crucial step of identifying avoidant patterns in your life. Avoidant attachment is often characterized by a reluctance to depend on others or to allow others to depend on you, stemming from a deep-seated fear of intimacy and vulnerability. People with avoidant attachment may appear self-sufficient, independent, and emotionally distant. They often maintain a façade of invulnerability, avoiding situations where they might feel emotionally exposed or where they might have to rely on someone else.

One of the primary signs of avoidant attachment is an aversion to closeness in relationships. This doesn't necessarily mean that individuals with avoidant attachment don't desire connections with others; rather, they feel discomfort and anxiety when relationships become too close or when emotional demands are placed on them. They might find themselves pulling away from partners when the relationship starts to deepen, often using work, hobbies, or other distractions as a means of maintaining emotional distance. This pattern of withdrawing from closeness can make it difficult for them to establish deep, meaningful relationships.

Another symptom of avoidant attachment is a tendency to suppress or ignore emotions, both their own and those of others. Individuals with avoidant attachment often struggle to express their feelings openly, preferring to keep their emotions private. They may downplay the importance of emotions, viewing them as a sign of weakness, and may have difficulty empathizing with others' emotional needs. This emotional suppression can lead to a lack of emotional intimacy in relationships, as their partners may feel that they are distant or unresponsive to their needs.

Avoidant attachment is also marked by a strong preference for independence and self-reliance. While independence is generally seen as a positive trait, in the context of avoidant attachment, it can become a barrier to forming close relationships. People with avoidant attachment often pride themselves on their ability to handle things on their own and may resist asking for help or support, even when they need it. This fierce independence can make it difficult for them to connect with others on a deeper level, as they may perceive reliance on others as a weakness.

Another common pattern associated with avoidant attachment is a fear of commitment. Individuals with avoidant attachment may struggle with the idea of long-term commitment, fearing that it will lead to a loss of personal freedom or that they will be trapped in a situation where their emotional needs will not be met. This fear can manifest in various ways, such as avoiding serious relationships, keeping partners at arm's length, or engaging in behaviors that sabotage the relationship when it starts to become too serious.

In addition to these behavioral patterns, individuals with avoidant attachment may also experience a lack of trust in others. This lack of trust can stem from early experiences where they learned that relying on others was either unsafe or unwise. As a result, they may be hesitant to let others get too close, fearing that they will be let down or betrayed. This mistrust can lead to a tendency to keep people at a distance, both emotionally and physically, and can contribute to the cycle of avoidance in relationships.

Understanding emotional distance and withdrawal is central to identifying avoidant attachment patterns. Emotional distance refers to the tendency to keep others at an emotional arm's length, avoiding intimacy and vulnerability. This distance can manifest in various ways, such as being unresponsive to a partner's emotional needs, avoiding discussions about feelings, or downplaying the significance of emotional events. Individuals with avoidant attachment often withdraw emotionally when they feel overwhelmed by the demands of a relationship, preferring to retreat into their own world rather than confront the discomfort of emotional closeness.

Withdrawal, in this context, doesn't necessarily mean physically leaving the relationship, though that can happen. More often, it involves creating an emotional barrier between themselves and their partner. This can include behaviors like becoming silent or uncommunicative during conflicts, avoiding eye contact, or physically distancing themselves by spending more time alone or away from the relationship. Emotional withdrawal can be deeply frustrating for their partners, who may feel shut out or rejected, leading to further strain in the relationship.

Another aspect of emotional distance is the tendency to intellectualize or rationalize emotions rather than experience them fully. Individuals with avoidant attachment might focus on the logical aspects of a situation, avoiding the emotional impact. For instance, they might downplay their partner's emotional concerns by focusing on practical solutions rather than acknowledging the emotional weight of the issue. This intellectualization can serve as a defense mechanism to avoid the vulnerability that comes with experiencing and expressing emotions.

Identifying these patterns in your life is the first step towards overcoming avoidant attachment. It requires a willingness to look honestly at your behaviors and the underlying fears that drive them. This self-awareness is crucial for breaking the cycle of avoidance and beginning the journey towards healthier, more secure relationships. Recognizing avoidant attachment patterns can be challenging, as they are often deeply ingrained and may feel like a natural or even necessary way of interacting with the world. However, with self-reflection and a commitment to growth, it is possible to move beyond these patterns and develop a more open and connected way of relating to others.

Identifying avoidant patterns in your life involves recognizing the signs and symptoms of avoidant attachment, understanding the role of emotional distance and withdrawal, and acknowledging the impact these patterns have on your relationships. By becoming aware of these behaviors, you can begin to challenge them and work towards building more fulfilling and secure connections with others. Overcoming avoidant attachment is a process that requires patience, self-compassion, and a willingness to embrace vulnerability, but it is a journey that can lead to deeper, more meaningful relationships and a greater sense of emotional fulfillment.

Steps to Reconnect Emotionally

Overcoming avoidant attachment involves not only recognizing the patterns that keep you emotionally distant but also taking proactive steps to reconnect emotionally with others. This process requires a commitment to personal growth and a willingness to embrace vulnerability, which is often the most challenging aspect for those with avoidant attachment. Emotional reconnection is not a one-time event but an ongoing journey that involves gradually opening up, building emotional intimacy, and fostering empathy and compassion in your relationships.

How to Open Up and Be Vulnerable

For individuals with avoidant attachment, opening up and being vulnerable can feel daunting. Vulnerability often feels like exposing oneself to potential hurt or rejection, which is why many people with avoidant tendencies shy away from it. However, vulnerability is essential for building deeper, more meaningful connections. The first step towards opening up is to start small. You don't have to share your deepest fears or most personal experiences right away. Begin by expressing your thoughts and feelings in less intimidating situations, such as sharing your opinion on a topic or discussing a minor concern.

It's also helpful to create a safe environment for vulnerability. This means finding a trusted person, whether it's a partner, friend, or therapist, who you feel comfortable with and who will listen without judgment. Start by sharing something small and gauge their response. If they respond with empathy and understanding, this can build your confidence to share more. Over time, as you practice being open in these smaller instances, it will become easier to be vulnerable in more significant areas of your life.

Another key to opening up is reframing your view of vulnerability. Instead of seeing it as a weakness or a risk, try to see it as a strength and a necessary part of emotional intimacy. Vulnerability allows others to see the real you and provides the opportunity for genuine connection. While there is always a risk of being hurt, the potential rewards of deeper, more fulfilling relationships are worth the effort. Remember that vulnerability is a two-way street; by being open yourself, you also encourage others to do the same, creating a mutually supportive relationship.

Building Emotional Intimacy and Trust

Building emotional intimacy is an essential step in overcoming avoidant attachment. Emotional intimacy goes beyond physical closeness; it involves sharing your inner world; your thoughts, feelings, fears, and dreams, with someone else. For those with avoidant attachment, this level of intimacy can feel overwhelming, but it's crucial for forming secure and lasting bonds.

One way to build emotional intimacy is through regular, open communication. Set aside time to talk with your partner or loved ones about how you're feeling, what's been on your mind, and any concerns or desires you have. These conversations don't have to be serious all the time; sharing joyful experiences, aspirations, or even everyday thoughts can also deepen your connection. The key is consistency; making it a habit to check in with each other emotionally helps to build a strong foundation of intimacy.

Trust is another cornerstone of emotional intimacy, and for those with avoidant attachment, building trust can be particularly challenging. Trust requires you to believe that others will support you emotionally and that they will not betray your vulnerabilities. To build trust, start by being reliable in your relationships; honor your commitments, be present when needed, and show consistency in your actions and words. Trust is built through positive, consistent experiences over time, so be patient with yourself and your relationships as you work to develop this trust.

The Role of Empathy and Compassion

Empathy and compassion play vital roles in reconnecting emotionally and overcoming avoidant attachment. Empathy allows you to understand and share the feelings of others, which is crucial for building deeper connections. When you can empathize with your partner or loved ones, you're better able to respond to their emotional needs and create a more supportive relationship.

For those with avoidant attachment, practicing empathy might not come naturally, as there may be a tendency to focus more on logic and independence than on emotional understanding. However, empathy can be cultivated with practice. Start by actively listening to others when they share their feelings, trying to put yourself in their shoes, and acknowledging their emotions. This doesn't mean you have to agree with everything they feel, but showing that you understand and respect their feelings can go a long way in fostering emotional closeness.

Compassion, on the other hand, involves a desire to alleviate the suffering of others and to offer support. In relationships, compassion means being there for your partner or loved ones when they're struggling, offering a kind word, a listening ear, or simply being present. It also involves self-compassion; recognizing your own emotional struggles and treating yourself with kindness and understanding rather than criticism. By cultivating both empathy and compassion, you can break down the barriers of avoidant attachment and create more emotionally fulfilling relationships.

Enhancing Relationship Satisfaction

The journey to overcoming avoidant attachment doesn't end with reconnecting emotionally; it also involves enhancing relationship satisfaction by learning to communicate your feelings, breaking down emotional walls, and reframing negative thoughts and beliefs that might be holding you back. These steps are crucial for not only maintaining healthy relationships but also for ensuring that those relationships are satisfying and rewarding for both you and your partner.

Learning to Communicate Your Feelings

Effective communication is essential for any relationship, but it is especially important for those working to overcome avoidant attachment. Learning to communicate your feelings clearly and openly can significantly enhance relationship satisfaction, as it fosters understanding and prevents misunderstandings. For those with avoidant tendencies, communicating feelings might feel uncomfortable or even unnecessary, but it's a vital skill to develop.

Start by practicing self-awareness, pay attention to your emotions and what triggers them. Once you have a clearer understanding of your feelings, practice expressing them in a way that is both honest and respectful. Use "I" statements to focus on your own experiences rather than placing blame or making assumptions about your partner's intentions. For example, instead of saying, "You never care about how I feel," you might say, "I feel hurt when my feelings seem overlooked."

It's also important to be patient with yourself as you develop these communication skills. If you're not used to talking about your emotions, it may feel awkward or difficult at first, but with practice, it will become easier. Remember that communication is not just about speaking; it's also about listening. Make an effort to truly hear your partner's feelings and perspectives, and respond with empathy and understanding. This two-way communication can greatly enhance relationship satisfaction and deepen your emotional connection.

Breaking Down Emotional Walls

Breaking down emotional walls is a critical part of overcoming avoidant attachment and enhancing relationship satisfaction. Emotional walls are the barriers you put up to protect yourself from potential hurt or vulnerability. While these walls might provide a sense of safety in the short term, they ultimately prevent you from experiencing the deep, meaningful connections that are essential for a fulfilling relationship.

To start breaking down these walls, you need to recognize when and why you put them up. Emotional walls often go up in response to fear; fear of being hurt, rejected, or overwhelmed by emotion. Understanding the root of these fears is the first step in addressing them. Once you've identified your fears, challenge them by gradually allowing yourself to be more open and vulnerable in your relationships.

Breaking down emotional walls also involves taking risks; being willing to let your guard down and trust that your partner will not take advantage of your vulnerability. This process takes time and should be done at a pace that feels manageable for you. It might involve sharing something personal about yourself, asking for help, or simply allowing yourself to rely on your partner more. With each small step, you build confidence in your ability to be open and emotionally available, which in turn enhances relationship satisfaction.

Reframing Negative Thoughts and Beliefs

Finally, overcoming avoidant attachment and enhancing relationship satisfaction requires reframing negative thoughts and beliefs that contribute to your avoidant patterns. These negative thoughts often stem from past experiences or deeply ingrained beliefs about yourself and relationships, such as the belief that relying on others is a sign of weakness, or that emotional intimacy will inevitably lead to hurt.

Reframing these thoughts involves challenging their validity and considering alternative, more positive perspectives. For instance, instead of thinking, "If I open up, I'll just get hurt," you might reframe this thought to, "Opening up allows me to build closer, more meaningful connections." This doesn't mean ignoring the risks associated with vulnerability, but rather acknowledging that the potential rewards, such as emotional closeness and relationship satisfaction, outweigh those risks.

Cognitive-behavioral techniques, such as thought records or cognitive restructuring, can be particularly helpful in identifying and reframing negative thoughts. By systematically challenging your negative beliefs and replacing them with more balanced, realistic thoughts, you can reduce the impact of avoidant attachment on your relationships and create a more positive, fulfilling relationship dynamic.

In conclusion, overcoming avoidant attachment and enhancing relationship satisfaction involves taking proactive steps to reconnect emotionally, communicate more effectively, break down emotional walls, and reframe negative thoughts and beliefs. By committing to these steps, you can transform your relationships into sources of deep emotional fulfillment and security. While the journey may be challenging, the rewards of healthier, more satisfying relationships are well worth the effort. Through self-awareness, empathy, and a willingness to embrace vulnerability, you can overcome avoidant attachment and create the

deep, meaningful connections that are essential for
a fulfilling life.

Chapter 5

Cultivating a Secure Attachment

Cultivating a secure attachment is the cornerstone of creating healthy, lasting relationships and fostering a sense of inner peace. For those transitioning from an insecure attachment style; whether anxious or avoidant, the journey toward secure attachment involves deliberate practice, self-awareness, and the development of new emotional habits. A secure attachment is characterized by a strong sense of self-worth, the ability to trust others, and the capacity to give and receive love freely. This chapter delves into the processes and practices necessary to cultivate a secure attachment, focusing on both internal growth and relational dynamics.

Transitioning from Insecure to Secure

The transition from an insecure attachment style to a secure one is not instantaneous but rather a gradual process that requires dedication and self-reflection. Developing secure attachment traits involves recognizing the patterns and behaviors that have kept you trapped in insecurity and replacing them with healthier, more adaptive responses. This transformation begins with understanding the traits of secure attachment, such as the ability to manage emotions, the capacity to communicate needs effectively, and the confidence to seek support when necessary.

One of the first steps in developing secure attachment traits is to challenge the negative beliefs that underpin your insecure attachment. For instance, if you have an anxious attachment, you might hold the belief that you are unworthy of love or that relationships inevitably lead to rejection. These beliefs fuel your anxiety and make it difficult to feel secure in relationships. By identifying these negative thoughts and actively challenging them, you can begin to shift your mindset towards one that supports secure attachment.

Another crucial aspect of transitioning to secure attachment is practicing self-compassion and self-love. Insecure attachment styles often arise from a lack of self-worth and a tendency to be overly critical of oneself. To cultivate a secure attachment, it is essential to develop a more compassionate relationship with yourself. This means treating yourself with kindness, acknowledging your strengths, and being forgiving of your mistakes. Self-compassion helps to build resilience, which is necessary for maintaining a secure attachment, especially during challenging times.

Rebuilding confidence in relationships is also vital for developing a secure attachment. This involves taking risks in your relationships, such as being vulnerable or expressing your needs, and trusting that others will respond with care and support. It's important to remember that building confidence doesn't mean expecting perfection from yourself or others; rather, it's about trusting in your ability to navigate relational challenges and learning from your experiences. Over time, as you experience positive outcomes from these risks, your confidence in relationships will grow, reinforcing your secure attachment.

The Importance of Mindfulness and Self-Care

Mindfulness and self-care are foundational practices for cultivating a secure attachment. These practices help you to stay grounded in the present moment, manage anxiety, and maintain emotional balance, all of which are essential for developing and sustaining secure attachment traits. Mindfulness, in particular, is a powerful tool for managing the emotional reactivity that often accompanies insecure attachment styles. By staying present and observing your thoughts and feelings without judgment, you can create a sense of emotional stability that supports secure attachment.

Mindfulness techniques to manage anxiety are especially useful for those transitioning from anxious attachment. Anxious individuals often struggle with racing thoughts, excessive worry, and a tendency to catastrophize, all of which can undermine their sense of security in relationships. Mindfulness practices, such as deep breathing exercises, body scans, and meditation, can help to calm the nervous system and bring your focus back to the present moment. These techniques allow you to observe your anxiety without getting caught up in it, giving you the space to respond to situations with greater clarity and calmness.

Creating a self-care routine for emotional balance is another key aspect of cultivating a secure attachment. Self-care involves more than just physical well-being; it encompasses taking care of your emotional, mental, and spiritual needs as well. A well-rounded self-care routine can help you to manage stress, regulate your emotions, and maintain a positive outlook, all of which contribute to a secure attachment. Your self-care routine might include activities such as journaling, spending time in nature, engaging in creative hobbies, practicing gratitude, or seeking support from a therapist or support group.

It's important to personalize your self-care routine to meet your specific needs and preferences. For example, if you tend to struggle with anxiety, you might prioritize calming activities such as meditation or yoga. If you find yourself feeling isolated or disconnected, you might focus on social self-care, such as spending quality time with loved ones or participating in community activities. The key is to consistently engage in self-care practices that nourish your emotional well-being and support your journey toward a secure attachment.

Mindfulness and self-care not only help you to manage your own emotions but also enhance your ability to connect with others in a healthy, secure way. When you are grounded and emotionally balanced, you are better equipped to handle relational challenges, communicate effectively, and maintain a sense of security within yourself. This, in turn, fosters secure attachment in your relationships, creating a positive feedback loop that reinforces your growth.

Cultivating a secure attachment is a multifaceted process that involves transitioning from insecure patterns, practicing self-compassion and self-love, and incorporating mindfulness and self-care into your daily life. By committing to these practices, you can develop the traits and behaviors that characterize secure attachment, leading to more fulfilling and harmonious relationships. While the journey may require patience and perseverance, the rewards of secure attachment; emotional stability, deeper connections, and a stronger sense of self, are well worth the effort. Through mindful awareness, self-compassion, and a dedication to personal growth, you can cultivate a secure attachment that will serve as the foundation for a life of emotional well-being and relational satisfaction.

Building and Maintaining Secure Relationships

Building and maintaining secure relationships is the culmination of cultivating secure attachment traits within yourself. Once you've established a strong foundation of self-compassion, mindfulness, and emotional balance, the next step is to extend these qualities into your relationships. A secure relationship is characterized by trust, open communication, mutual respect, and a deep sense of connection. These relationships don't just happen; they require ongoing effort, intentionality, and a commitment to nurturing both the relationship and the individuals within it.

How to Nurture Security with Your Partner

Nurturing security in a relationship begins with creating a safe space for both partners to express themselves authentically. This involves open and honest communication, where each person feels heard and understood. One way to foster this kind of communication is by practicing active listening; truly paying attention to your partner's words, emotions, and non-verbal cues without interrupting or preparing your response while they speak. This kind of attentiveness shows your partner that you value their thoughts and feelings, which is fundamental to building trust and security.

Another crucial aspect of nurturing security with your partner is the willingness to be vulnerable. Vulnerability is often seen as a risk, especially for those with avoidant attachment tendencies, but it is essential for deepening intimacy and connection. Sharing your fears, hopes, and dreams with your partner, and encouraging them to do the same, can strengthen the emotional bond between you. Vulnerability allows for a deeper understanding of each other, which helps to build a more secure and resilient relationship.

It's also important to practice emotional attunement; being in tune with your partner's emotional state and responding with empathy and support. Emotional attunement involves recognizing when your partner is feeling stressed, anxious, or upset, and offering comfort or assistance. This doesn't mean solving their problems for them, but rather being present and offering emotional support, which reinforces the sense of security in the relationship.

The Role of Mutual Support and Respect

Mutual support and respect are the cornerstones of any secure relationship. Supporting your partner means being there for them in both good times and bad, offering encouragement and understanding, and celebrating their successes. It's about recognizing that a relationship is a partnership where both individuals contribute to each other's well-being. This support should be reciprocal; both partners should feel that they can rely on each other for emotional and practical support.

Respect in a relationship involves honoring each other's boundaries, values, and individuality. It means acknowledging your partner's perspective, even when it differs from your own, and refraining from behaviors that might undermine their self-esteem or autonomy. Respect also entails recognizing and appreciating the strengths and qualities that your partner brings to the relationship. This appreciation fosters a positive dynamic where both partners feel valued and respected, which is essential for maintaining security.

In secure relationships, conflicts are approached with mutual respect rather than defensiveness or blame. When disagreements arise, secure partners focus on resolving the issue at hand without attacking each other's character. They engage in constructive dialogue, seek to understand each other's viewpoints, and work together to find a solution. This respectful approach to conflict not only preserves the relationship but also strengthens it, as both partners learn to navigate challenges in a way that reinforces their bond.

Long-Term Strategies for Relationship Growth

Maintaining a secure relationship over the long term requires ongoing effort and a commitment to growth. One effective strategy for sustaining relationship growth is to continually invest in your connection with your partner. This might involve setting aside regular time for each other, whether it's through date nights, weekend getaways, or simply spending quality time together at home. These moments of connection help to keep the relationship strong and prevent it from becoming stagnant.

Another long-term strategy is to practice gratitude regularly. Taking the time to express appreciation for your partner's actions, qualities, and the relationship itself can significantly enhance the sense of security and satisfaction in the relationship. Gratitude fosters a positive atmosphere and helps both partners to focus on the strengths of the relationship rather than its shortcomings.

It's also important to support each other's personal growth. In secure relationships, both partners encourage each other to pursue their individual goals and passions. This support might involve offering encouragement, providing practical assistance, or simply respecting each other's need for time and space to focus on personal development. When both partners feel that their personal growth is valued within the relationship, they are more likely to remain committed and engaged over the long term.

Finally, maintaining a secure relationship involves being adaptable and open to change. As individuals grow and evolve, so too must the relationship. This might mean adjusting to new life circumstances, redefining roles within the relationship, or exploring new ways of connecting. By being flexible and willing to adapt, secure partners can navigate life's changes together, ensuring that their relationship remains strong and supportive.

In conclusion, building and maintaining secure relationships is an ongoing process that requires intentional effort, mutual support, and a commitment to growth. By nurturing security through open communication, vulnerability, and emotional attunement, partners can create a strong foundation for their relationship. Mutual support and respect further reinforce this foundation, fostering a positive and healthy dynamic. Long-term strategies, such as investing in the relationship, practicing gratitude, supporting personal growth, and remaining adaptable, ensure that the relationship continues to thrive over time. With these practices, you can cultivate a secure and fulfilling relationship that brings lasting happiness and satisfaction.

Chapter 6

Practical Exercises and Tools

The journey toward healing and cultivating a secure attachment is deeply personal and transformative. However, this journey isn't solely based on intellectual understanding; it also requires active engagement and practical exercises that help integrate these concepts into your daily life. Practical exercises and tools like journaling and meditation are instrumental in deepening self-awareness, healing emotional wounds, and reinforcing the secure attachment traits you aim to cultivate. This chapter delves into two powerful practices; journaling and guided meditation, that can serve as vital resources on your path to emotional healing and relational security.

Journaling Prompts for Self-Discovery

Journaling is a profoundly effective tool for self-discovery and emotional processing. It offers a private space to explore your thoughts, feelings, and experiences, allowing you to uncover insights that might otherwise remain hidden in your subconscious. When it comes to understanding and healing attachment styles, journaling can help you explore your attachment history, recognize patterns in your relationships, and track your progress toward a more secure attachment style.

Exploring your attachment history is one of the most crucial steps in understanding your current relational patterns. Many of the attachment behaviors we exhibit in adulthood stem from early experiences with caregivers. By journaling about your childhood relationships, specifically, the ways in which your caregivers responded to your needs, how you felt about their responses, and the impact these experiences had on you, you can begin to identify the roots of your attachment style. For instance, if you had caregivers who were inconsistent in their emotional availability, you might notice a pattern of anxiety in your adult relationships, constantly seeking reassurance to compensate for the insecurity you felt as a child.

Another valuable aspect of journaling for self-discovery is reflecting on your relationship patterns. This involves examining your past and present relationships to identify recurring themes and behaviors. For example, if you tend to push people away when they get too close, you might uncover a pattern of avoidant attachment. By writing about these patterns, you can start to see the connections between your past experiences and your current relationship behaviors. This awareness is the first step toward changing these patterns and fostering more secure relationships.

Journaling also provides an opportunity to document your progress as you work on developing a secure attachment. By regularly writing about your thoughts, feelings, and interactions, you can observe changes in your behavior and emotional responses over time. This can be incredibly encouraging, as it allows you to see how far you've come and reinforces your commitment to personal growth. Moreover, journaling can help you process any setbacks or challenges you encounter along the way, providing a constructive outlet for your emotions and helping you to stay focused on your goals.

Guided Meditations for Emotional Healing

While journaling is a powerful tool for self-reflection, guided meditation offers a different, yet equally valuable, pathway to emotional healing. Meditation helps to calm the mind, reduce stress, and promote a sense of inner peace; essential qualities for cultivating a secure attachment. Guided meditations, in particular, are designed to lead you through specific mental exercises that can help you heal attachment-related wounds, manage anxiety, and develop emotional balance.

Meditations to reduce anxiety and promote security are particularly beneficial for individuals with anxious attachment. Anxiety often manifests as a constant fear of abandonment or rejection, leading to behaviors that can strain relationships. Guided meditations that focus on grounding and calming the nervous system can help to alleviate these feelings of anxiety. For example, a meditation that emphasizes deep breathing and visualization of a safe, comforting space can help you to relax and release the tension that fuels anxious thoughts. Over time, practicing such meditations regularly can help to rewire your brain, making it easier to remain calm and secure in your relationships.

In addition to reducing anxiety, guided meditations can also help you cultivate a greater sense of security within yourself. This might involve meditations that encourage you to connect with your inner strength and resilience. By visualizing yourself as a strong, capable, and loving individual, you can begin to internalize these qualities, which in turn can help you develop a more secure attachment style. These meditations can also include affirmations that reinforce your self-worth and your ability to create and maintain healthy relationships.

Visualization techniques for emotional balance are another powerful aspect of guided meditation. These techniques involve creating mental images that evoke feelings of peace, security, and emotional balance. For instance, you might visualize a serene landscape where you feel completely at ease, or imagine a warm, loving light surrounding you, filling you with a sense of safety and comfort. Visualization helps to anchor positive emotions in your mind and body, making it easier to access these feelings in your daily life. By regularly practicing visualization, you can train your brain to shift away from patterns of fear and insecurity, and toward a state of emotional balance and well-being.

Guided meditations can also be tailored to address specific emotional wounds related to attachment. For example, if you struggle with feelings of unworthiness or fear of rejection, you might choose meditations that focus on healing these specific issues. Such meditations could involve visualizing yourself as a child receiving unconditional love and support, or imagining a future where you are fully embraced and accepted in your relationships. By repeatedly engaging in these visualizations, you can begin to heal the emotional scars that contribute to insecure attachment.

Practical exercises like journaling and guided meditation are invaluable tools on the journey to healing and cultivating a secure attachment. Journaling offers a space for deep self-reflection, allowing you to explore your attachment history, recognize patterns in your relationships, and document your progress. Guided meditations, on the other hand, provide a pathway to emotional healing, helping you to reduce anxiety, develop a sense of security, and maintain emotional balance. By integrating these practices into your daily routine, you can actively work toward transforming your attachment style and creating healthier, more fulfilling relationships. The journey may be challenging at times, but with the right tools and a commitment to growth, you can achieve a secure attachment and the emotional well-being that comes with it.

Role-Playing Scenarios for Relationship Improvement

Role-playing is a dynamic and interactive exercise that can significantly enhance your ability to navigate relationships with greater empathy, understanding, and effective communication. This technique involves acting out various scenarios that you might encounter in your relationships, allowing you to practice and refine your responses in a safe and controlled environment. Role-playing not only helps you to better understand your own emotional triggers and behaviors but also fosters a deeper understanding of your partner's perspective. By repeatedly practicing these scenarios, you can develop the skills necessary to improve your relationships and cultivate a more secure attachment style.

Practicing Effective Communication

Effective communication is the cornerstone of any healthy relationship, but it can be particularly challenging for individuals with insecure attachment styles. For those with anxious attachment, the fear of abandonment can lead to over-communicating, seeking constant reassurance, or misinterpreting neutral or ambiguous statements as signs of rejection. Conversely, individuals with avoidant attachment might struggle with opening up, often keeping their thoughts and feelings to themselves out of a fear of vulnerability. Role-playing provides a valuable opportunity to practice and improve communication skills in a way that addresses these attachment-related challenges.

In role-playing scenarios focused on communication, you can simulate conversations that you might find difficult in real life. For example, if you often struggle with expressing your needs or setting boundaries, you can role-play a situation where you clearly and assertively communicate your desires or limits to your partner. This exercise allows you to practice finding the right words, tone, and body language that convey your message effectively without resorting to aggression or passivity. Through repeated practice, you can build confidence in your ability to communicate assertively and respectfully, which is essential for fostering security in relationships.

Additionally, role-playing can help you develop strategies for managing conflict in a way that strengthens your relationship rather than undermines it. Conflicts are inevitable in any relationship, but how they are handled can either reinforce or erode the bond between partners. In a role-playing scenario, you might practice responding to a disagreement with calmness and empathy, rather than reacting defensively or withdrawing. This could involve using "I" statements to express your feelings without blaming your partner, actively listening to their perspective, and working together to find a mutually acceptable solution. By rehearsing these techniques, you can become more adept at navigating conflicts in a way that promotes understanding and resolution, rather than escalation.

Building Empathy and Understanding

Empathy; the ability to understand and share the feelings of another, is a crucial component of healthy and secure relationships. For those working to overcome avoidant or anxious attachment, developing empathy can help bridge the emotional distance that often characterizes these attachment styles. Role-playing is an effective tool for building empathy because it allows you to step into another person's shoes and experience the situation from their perspective.

In role-playing exercises designed to build empathy, you might switch roles with your partner or another participant. For example, if you are typically the one who withdraws during conflicts, you could take on the role of the partner who feels abandoned or rejected when this happens. By experiencing the situation from the other side, you gain a deeper understanding of how your actions affect others and why they might react in certain ways. This increased empathy can help you to be more compassionate and patient in real-life interactions, reducing misunderstandings and fostering a stronger emotional connection.

Another way role-playing can enhance empathy is by practicing active listening, a skill that is vital for truly understanding your partner's needs and emotions. In a role-playing scenario, you could practice responding to your partner's concerns by reflecting back what they've said, validating their feelings, and asking open-ended questions to encourage further dialogue. This not only demonstrates that you are listening and care about their perspective but also helps to deepen your connection by showing that you value their experience. Over time, practicing active listening in role-playing scenarios can translate into more empathetic and supportive communication in your everyday interactions.

Role-playing can also be used to rehearse responses to challenging situations where empathy is crucial. For instance, if your partner is expressing vulnerability or distress, you can practice responding with warmth, understanding, and reassurance, rather than defensiveness or dismissal. This practice helps to condition your emotional responses, making it more likely that you will react with empathy and compassion when similar situations arise in real life.

In summary, role-playing scenarios for relationship improvement are a powerful tool for enhancing both communication and empathy, two essential ingredients for secure attachment. By practicing effective communication, you can learn to express your needs, set boundaries, and manage conflicts in a way that strengthens your relationships. At the same time, role-playing allows you to build empathy by seeing situations from your partner's perspective and practicing active listening. Together, these skills can help you to overcome the challenges of insecure attachment, fostering healthier, more fulfilling relationships. Through consistent practice and application of these techniques, you can develop the emotional intelligence and relational skills necessary to create and maintain secure, supportive, and loving connections.

Chapter 7

Relationship Dynamics and Attachment Styles

Understanding how attachment styles interact within relationships is crucial for navigating the complex dynamics that arise between partners. Attachment styles, which are often formed in early childhood, significantly influence how individuals behave in romantic relationships, especially in times of conflict or emotional stress. These styles can create a unique interplay of needs, fears, and behaviors that shape the overall health and stability of the relationship. In this chapter, we explore how different attachment styles interact, the specific challenges and solutions for anxious-avoidant relationships, and strategies for navigating conflict and creating harmony, regardless of the attachment styles involved.

How Attachment Styles Interact in Relationships

One of the most common and challenging dynamics in relationships involves the interaction between anxious and avoidant attachment styles. This pairing, often referred to as the anxious-avoidant trap, creates a push-and-pull dynamic that can be emotionally exhausting for both partners. Individuals with anxious attachment tend to crave closeness and reassurance, often fearing abandonment. In contrast, those with avoidant attachment value independence and may become uncomfortable with too much closeness, leading them to withdraw emotionally. This combination can lead to a cycle where the anxious partner pursues connection, causing the avoidant partner to pull away, which in turn heightens the anxious partner's fears and intensifies their pursuit. This cycle can be incredibly difficult to break without conscious effort and understanding from both parties.

The challenges of anxious-avoidant relationships stem from the fundamental differences in how each partner approaches intimacy and conflict. For the anxious partner, the avoidant's withdrawal can feel like rejection or abandonment, triggering feelings of insecurity and anxiety. They may respond by becoming more clingy, demanding, or emotionally expressive in an attempt to draw their partner closer. However, these behaviors often have the opposite effect, as the avoidant partner may feel overwhelmed or suffocated by the intensity of the anxious partner's emotions, leading them to retreat further. This creates a vicious cycle where neither partner's needs are fully met, and both may feel frustrated, misunderstood, and disconnected.

The solution to this dynamic lies in both partners developing a deeper understanding of their own attachment styles and how these influence their behaviors in the relationship. The anxious partner can work on developing self-soothing techniques and building their self-esteem outside of the relationship, reducing their reliance on their partner for reassurance. Meanwhile, the avoidant partner can practice being more emotionally available and communicative, recognizing that their partner's needs for closeness are valid and not necessarily a threat to their independence. Open, honest communication about needs, fears, and boundaries is essential in these relationships to break the cycle and create a more balanced dynamic.

Mixed attachment styles in relationships, where each partner has a different attachment style, can also create a range of challenges. For example, a relationship between a securely attached individual and an anxious or avoidant partner might involve different dynamics. The securely attached partner may struggle to understand why their anxious partner needs constant reassurance or why their avoidant partner prefers emotional distance. However, their secure attachment style can also be a stabilizing force in the relationship, offering a model of healthy attachment that can help their partner develop more secure behaviors over time. The key to navigating mixed attachment styles is for each partner to be patient, empathetic, and committed to understanding and supporting each other's emotional needs.

Navigating Conflict and Creating Harmony

Conflict is a natural part of any relationship, but how it is handled can either strengthen or weaken the bond between partners, especially when different attachment styles are at play. Each attachment style has its own way of dealing with conflict, which can sometimes exacerbate misunderstandings and lead to unresolved issues if not addressed appropriately. Developing effective conflict resolution strategies that take into account the unique needs and behaviors of each attachment style is crucial for maintaining harmony in the relationship.

For anxious individuals, conflict can be particularly distressing, as it may trigger fears of abandonment or rejection. They might respond to conflict by becoming overly emotional, seeking immediate resolution, or excessively apologizing to avoid losing their partner. To navigate conflict effectively, it is important for the anxious partner to practice self-regulation techniques, such as deep breathing or taking a time-out to calm down before discussing the issue. It is equally important for their partner to acknowledge and validate their feelings, rather than dismissing them, which can help to reassure the anxious partner and de-escalate the situation.

Avoidant individuals, on the other hand, may respond to conflict by withdrawing or shutting down emotionally, as they tend to view conflict as a threat to their autonomy. They might avoid discussing the issue altogether, hoping it will resolve itself without confrontation. However, this approach can lead to unresolved tensions and resentment over time. For avoidant partners, it is important to recognize that conflict is a normal and necessary part of relationships and that addressing issues openly can actually strengthen the bond rather than diminish it. They can work on gradually becoming more comfortable with expressing their feelings and needs, even when it feels uncomfortable or vulnerable.

Creating a supportive and safe relationship environment is essential for all attachment styles to thrive. This involves cultivating an atmosphere of mutual respect, trust, and empathy, where both partners feel heard, valued, and understood. One effective strategy for creating such an environment is to establish regular check-ins, where both partners can openly discuss their feelings, concerns, and any issues that have arisen without the pressure of immediate conflict resolution. These check-ins can help to prevent small issues from escalating into major conflicts and provide a space for each partner to express their needs and emotions in a calm and supportive setting.

In addition to regular communication, it is important for both partners to practice active listening, where they fully focus on what the other person is saying without interrupting, judging, or planning their response. This helps to ensure that both partners feel understood and respected, even if they do not always agree on the issue at hand. Empathy plays a crucial role in this process, as it allows each partner to put themselves in the other's shoes and appreciate their perspective, even if it differs from their own.

Long-term relationship growth depends on the consistent application of these strategies and a willingness to adapt and learn from each other. By embracing the differences in attachment styles and working together to create a harmonious relationship environment, couples can build a strong, secure, and lasting bond. The journey toward creating harmony in a relationship with differing attachment styles requires patience, effort, and a commitment to growth.

The Role of Therapy and Professional Support

While self-awareness, effective communication, and relationship-building strategies are vital tools for managing and healing attachment styles, there are times when professional support becomes essential. Therapy can offer an invaluable space for individuals and couples to explore the roots of their attachment issues, understand their emotional patterns, and develop healthier ways of relating to themselves and others. For many, therapy is not just a tool for resolving immediate relationship problems but a long-term investment in emotional well-being and personal growth. This section will delve into when it might be time to seek help from a therapist and the various types of therapy that can be particularly effective in healing attachment issues.

When to Seek Help from a Therapist

Understanding when to seek therapy can be challenging, especially in relationships where attachment styles have created deeply ingrained patterns of behavior. However, certain signs may indicate that professional help could be beneficial. If you or your partner consistently struggle with intense emotions such as anxiety, fear of abandonment, or difficulty trusting one another, these may be symptoms of underlying attachment issues that require more than self-help strategies. Other indicators include recurring conflicts that remain unresolved, feelings of emotional disconnection or loneliness despite being in a relationship, and persistent patterns of unhealthy or destructive behavior, such as avoidance, withdrawal, or excessive clinginess.

For those with anxious attachment, therapy can help address the deep-seated fears of rejection and abandonment that often drive their behaviors. If you find yourself constantly seeking reassurance from your partner, feeling overly dependent on their validation, or experiencing overwhelming anxiety in relationships, a therapist can help you explore the origins of these feelings and work on building a stronger sense of self-worth and emotional independence. Therapy can also help you develop healthier ways to express your needs and manage your emotions without becoming overwhelmed by fear or insecurity.

For individuals with avoidant attachment, therapy can be instrumental in addressing the fear of vulnerability and intimacy that often leads to emotional withdrawal. If you notice a pattern of distancing yourself from your partner, avoiding emotional conversations, or feeling uncomfortable with closeness, therapy can provide a safe space to explore these behaviors and the fears that underlie them. A therapist can help you work on gradually becoming more open and emotionally available, fostering deeper connections and a greater sense of security in your relationships.

Couples therapy can be particularly beneficial when both partners are struggling with attachment issues that are affecting their relationship. In a therapeutic setting, couples can learn to understand each other's attachment styles, communicate more effectively, and develop strategies for resolving conflicts in a way that strengthens their bond rather than erodes it. A therapist can guide couples in identifying and breaking unhealthy patterns, fostering a more secure and supportive relationship environment.

Types of Therapy for Healing Attachment Issues

Several therapeutic approaches have been shown to be effective in addressing attachment issues, each offering different tools and techniques to help individuals and couples heal. One of the most widely recognized methods is Attachment-Based Therapy, which focuses specifically on understanding and healing attachment wounds that originate in early childhood. This approach helps clients explore their early relationships with caregivers, understand how these experiences have shaped their attachment styles, and work on developing more secure attachment patterns in their current relationships.

Cognitive Behavioral Therapy (CBT) is another common approach that can be highly effective for individuals dealing with anxious or avoidant attachment. CBT helps clients identify and challenge the negative thought patterns and beliefs that contribute to their attachment behaviors, such as the fear of abandonment or the need for emotional distance. By reframing these thoughts and learning new ways of thinking, individuals can begin to change their behaviors and develop healthier, more secure attachment styles.

For those who have experienced trauma, which often plays a significant role in the development of insecure attachment, Trauma-Focused Therapy can be particularly beneficial. Approaches such as Eye Movement Desensitization and Reprocessing (EMDR) or Trauma-Informed Cognitive Behavioral Therapy (T-CBT) help individuals process and heal from traumatic experiences that may be contributing to their attachment issues. These therapies focus on reducing the emotional impact of trauma and developing new coping mechanisms that allow for healthier relationships.

Emotionally Focused Therapy (EFT) is another highly effective approach, particularly for couples dealing with attachment-related challenges. EFT focuses on identifying and transforming the emotional responses that drive negative interaction patterns in relationships. By helping couples understand and articulate their underlying emotional needs, EFT fosters greater emotional connection and security. This approach is particularly useful for couples who struggle with the anxious-avoidant dynamic, as it helps both partners develop a deeper understanding of each other's attachment needs and fears.

Mindfulness-Based Therapy is also gaining recognition for its effectiveness in helping individuals with insecure attachment. This approach encourages clients to develop greater self-awareness and emotional regulation through mindfulness practices. By learning to observe their thoughts and feelings without judgment, individuals can gain insight into their attachment behaviors and learn to respond to relationship challenges with greater calmness and clarity.

In some cases, a combination of therapies may be the most effective approach. For example, a therapist might use CBT to help a client challenge negative thought patterns while also incorporating mindfulness techniques to improve emotional regulation. Similarly, a couple might engage in EFT to strengthen their emotional connection while also participating in individual therapy to address personal attachment issues.

Therapy is not a quick fix but a journey toward greater self-awareness, emotional resilience, and healthier relationships. It requires commitment, openness, and a willingness to explore and challenge deeply ingrained patterns. However, the benefits of therapy can be profound, leading to lasting changes in how individuals relate to themselves and others. Whether you are struggling with anxious or avoidant attachment, or simply seeking to strengthen your relationship, therapy offers a path toward healing, growth, and the development of secure, fulfilling relationships.

Chapter 8

Moving Forward: Creating a New Attachment Story

As you progress in your journey of understanding and healing your attachment style, the next critical step is to embrace the possibility of change and growth. This chapter focuses on the process of rewriting your attachment narrative, transitioning from patterns that may have caused pain or dysfunction to those that promote healthy, secure relationships. It's about moving forward with the awareness and tools you've gained, and committing to the ongoing work of self-discovery and healing. Creating a new attachment story isn't just about changing behaviors; it's about transforming how you see yourself and how you engage with others, allowing for deeper, more meaningful connections.

Embracing Change and Growth

Change is often challenging, especially when it involves altering deeply ingrained patterns that have been part of your life for many years. For those with anxious or avoidant attachment styles, these patterns may have provided a sense of safety or predictability, even if they also brought about pain or frustration. Embracing change requires a willingness to step out of your comfort zone and face the vulnerabilities that come with forming new, healthier habits. It involves recognizing that while these old patterns served a purpose at one point, they no longer support your growth or well-being. The process of change is not linear and may involve setbacks, but each step forward is an important part of your healing journey.

Rewriting your attachment narrative begins with the understanding that you are not bound by the attachment style you developed in childhood. While early experiences with caregivers play a significant role in shaping your attachment style, these patterns are not fixed and can be reshaped through conscious effort and self-awareness. This process often starts with reflecting on your past relationships and identifying the recurring themes or behaviors that have impacted your connections with others. By recognizing these patterns, you can begin to understand how they were formed and how they have influenced your relationships. This awareness is the first step in creating a new story, one where you have the power to choose how you relate to others and yourself.

The process of rewriting your attachment narrative also involves setting new intentions for your relationships. What do you want to change? What kind of connections do you want to build moving forward? These intentions serve as a guide for your actions and decisions, helping you stay focused on your goal of developing a more secure attachment style. It's important to be patient and compassionate with yourself during this process, as change takes time and requires practice. You may find that old patterns resurface, especially during times of stress or emotional difficulty. Rather than seeing these moments as failures, view them as opportunities to learn and grow. Each time you catch yourself falling back into old habits, you have the chance to choose a different path, reinforcing your commitment to change.

Staying committed to healing is essential as you work to create a new attachment story. This commitment involves both internal and external efforts. Internally, it means continuing to engage in self-reflection and self-awareness practices, such as journaling or meditation, that help you stay connected to your emotions and motivations. These practices allow you to monitor your progress and make adjustments as needed, ensuring that you remain aligned with your goals. Externally, commitment to healing involves maintaining the relationships and support systems that nurture your growth. Surrounding yourself with people who encourage and support your journey can make a significant difference, providing the emotional safety and encouragement needed to persevere.

Another important aspect of embracing change and growth is learning to trust the process. Healing and developing a secure attachment style is a journey that doesn't have a definitive endpoint. There will be times when progress feels slow or even non-existent, but trust that each effort you make contributes to your overall growth. Over time, the small changes you implement in your daily interactions and thought patterns will accumulate, leading to significant transformations in how you relate to others and yourself. This trust in the process also means accepting that healing is not about achieving perfection but about continuous improvement and self-discovery.

One of the key challenges in creating a new attachment story is dealing with the fear of vulnerability that often accompanies change. For those with avoidant attachment, vulnerability can feel particularly daunting, as it may be associated with the loss of control or independence. However, embracing vulnerability is essential for forming deeper connections and developing a secure attachment style. It involves allowing yourself to be seen and known by others, even when it feels uncomfortable. This doesn't mean exposing yourself to harm or abandoning your boundaries, but rather learning to share your authentic self with those you trust, creating a foundation for genuine intimacy and trust.

For individuals with anxious attachment, embracing change may involve learning to tolerate uncertainty and resist the urge to seek constant reassurance. This process can be uncomfortable, as it requires facing the fear of abandonment and learning to self-soothe in moments of anxiety. Over time, however, this practice can lead to a stronger sense of self-worth and emotional independence, reducing the need for external validation and allowing for healthier, more balanced relationships.

Ultimately, creating a new attachment story is about reclaiming your narrative and taking control of how you want to experience relationships. It's about moving away from reactive, fear-based patterns and towards intentional, love-based behaviors. This transformation requires effort, patience, and a deep commitment to yourself, but the rewards; a life filled with meaningful, secure connections, are well worth it.

As you move forward on this journey, remember that every step you take, no matter how small, is a victory. Each time you choose to respond differently in a relationship, to open up instead of withdrawing, or to soothe your own anxieties rather than seeking reassurance, you are rewriting your attachment story. This process is not about erasing the past but about integrating your experiences into a new, healthier narrative. It's about acknowledging where you've come from, understanding the impact of your early relationships, and deciding how you want to move forward.

In creating a new attachment story, you are not only transforming your relationships but also redefining your relationship with yourself. This journey of growth and healing is one of the most profound gifts you can give yourself, leading to a life that is richer, more connected, and deeply fulfilling. The work is ongoing, but with each step, you are building a foundation for a future where secure, loving relationships are not just possible but a reality.

Building Resilience and Emotional Strength

As you embark on the journey of rewriting your attachment narrative, building resilience and emotional strength becomes essential. This process is not just about making changes in the short term but developing the capacity to handle setbacks and challenges as they arise. Resilience, in this context, is the ability to bounce back from difficulties, learn from experiences, and continue moving forward despite obstacles. Emotional strength is the foundation that allows you to face your fears, regulate your emotions, and stay committed to your healing journey.

One of the key strategies for building resilience is learning to reframe setbacks not as failures but as opportunities for growth. Setbacks are an inevitable part of any personal development journey, especially when it involves changing deeply ingrained patterns like attachment styles. When you encounter a setback, whether it's falling back into old behaviors, experiencing emotional distress, or facing relationship difficulties, view it as a learning experience. Ask yourself what triggered the setback, how you responded, and what you can do differently next time. This process of reflection allows you to gain insights into your patterns and develop new strategies for handling similar situations in the future.

Cultivating patience is another crucial aspect of building resilience. Healing and personal growth take time, and it's important to recognize that progress may be slow and incremental. Patience involves accepting that change is a gradual process and that it's normal to experience ups and downs along the way. It's about giving yourself the time and space needed to fully integrate new behaviors and ways of thinking. When you practice patience, you create an environment of self-compassion, where you can acknowledge your progress without placing unrealistic expectations on yourself.

Persistence is closely linked to both resilience and patience. It's the determination to keep going, even when the journey is challenging or when you don't see immediate results. Persistence means committing to your healing process and maintaining your efforts over the long term. It involves continuing to practice new behaviors, even when they feel uncomfortable or unfamiliar, and sticking with the tools and strategies that support your growth. Over time, this persistence pays off, leading to lasting change and a more secure attachment style.

Building resilience and emotional strength also requires a focus on self-care. Self-care is not just about physical well-being but also about nurturing your emotional and mental health. This includes practices like mindfulness, which can help you stay grounded and present during difficult times, as well as activities that bring you joy and relaxation. Regular self-care helps to replenish your emotional reserves, making it easier to handle challenges and maintain your commitment to healing.

Another strategy for building resilience is to develop a strong support network. Surrounding yourself with people who understand your journey and offer encouragement can make a significant difference in your ability to stay resilient. This network might include friends, family, a therapist, or support groups. Having others to turn to during difficult times provides both emotional support and practical advice, helping you navigate setbacks and continue moving forward.

Ultimately, building resilience and emotional strength is about developing the tools and mindset needed to navigate life's challenges while staying true to your goals. It's about learning to trust yourself and your ability to handle whatever comes your way. With resilience and emotional strength, you can approach setbacks not as insurmountable obstacles but as part of the journey toward a more secure and fulfilling life.

Living with Secure Attachment

Living with a secure attachment style is transformative, impacting not only your relationships but also your overall sense of well-being and fulfillment. When you achieve a secure attachment, you experience a profound shift in how you relate to others and yourself. This section explores what life looks like with a secure attachment and how to maintain emotional balance and security over the long term.

With a secure attachment, relationships become a source of stability, support, and mutual respect. Instead of being driven by fear, anxiety, or avoidance, you approach relationships with confidence and openness. You feel comfortable expressing your needs and emotions, knowing that they will be met with understanding and care. This creates a foundation of trust and intimacy, where both partners feel safe and valued. In secure relationships, conflicts are handled with empathy and respect, leading to constructive resolutions rather than emotional turmoil. There is a sense of partnership and collaboration, where both individuals work together to build and maintain a healthy, loving relationship.

One of the most significant changes that come with secure attachment is the ability to regulate your emotions effectively. Instead of being overwhelmed by anxiety or fear, you can manage your emotions in a way that supports your well-being. This emotional regulation allows you to stay calm and centered, even in the face of challenges or disagreements. You no longer rely on external validation to feel secure; instead, you have a strong sense of self-worth and confidence in your ability to handle whatever comes your way. This inner stability is one of the hallmarks of secure attachment, providing a solid foundation for all aspects of your life.

Living with secure attachment also means experiencing a greater sense of balance in your life. Relationships are no longer a source of stress or instability but contribute to your overall happiness and well-being. You can enjoy deep, meaningful connections with others while also maintaining your independence and sense of self. This balance allows you to pursue your personal goals and interests without feeling the need to compromise your relationships. It's a state of harmony where your emotional needs are met, and you can thrive both individually and within your partnerships.

Maintaining emotional balance and security over the long term requires ongoing effort and awareness. Even with a secure attachment, it's important to continue practicing the skills and strategies that helped you achieve this state. This includes regular self-reflection, where you check in with yourself to ensure that you are staying aligned with your values and goals. It also involves continuing to communicate openly and honestly in your relationships, addressing any issues as they arise before they have the chance to escalate.

Mindfulness and self-care remain crucial practices for maintaining a secure attachment. By staying mindful of your thoughts and emotions, you can quickly identify any areas where you may be slipping back into old patterns. Self-care ensures that you are regularly replenishing your emotional reserves, keeping you balanced and resilient. Together, these practices help you maintain the emotional stability and confidence that define secure attachment.

Another key aspect of maintaining secure attachment is the willingness to grow and adapt. Life is dynamic, and relationships evolve over time. Staying open to change and being willing to adjust your approach as needed is essential for keeping your relationships healthy and fulfilling. This might involve learning new communication skills, exploring different ways to connect with your partner, or addressing any new challenges that arise. By staying flexible and responsive, you can ensure that your relationships continue to thrive.

Finally, living with secure attachment is about enjoying the richness and depth that comes with healthy, secure relationships. It's about feeling connected, loved, and supported, and being able to offer the same to others. It's a state of emotional security where you can fully embrace life's experiences, knowing that you have the strength and resilience to handle whatever comes your way. With secure attachment, you are not just surviving; you are thriving, living a life that is full of connection, joy, and fulfillment.

Conclusion

As you reach the conclusion of this exploration into attachment styles and their profound impact on your life, it is important to take a moment to reflect on the journey you have undertaken. This journey has been one of self-discovery, healing, and transformation, a path that has led you to a deeper understanding of yourself and your relationships. Reflecting on your journey involves acknowledging the progress you have made, the insights you have gained, and the growth you have experienced. It is a moment to celebrate your courage in facing your fears, confronting your past, and committing to change.

Throughout this process, you have explored the origins of your attachment style, identified the patterns that have shaped your relationships, and learned strategies to develop a more secure attachment. You have recognized the impact of your early experiences on your current behavior and have taken steps to heal the wounds that have influenced your life. This journey has not been easy; it has required vulnerability, self-reflection, and a willingness to confront uncomfortable truths. But it has also been a journey of empowerment, as you have gained the tools and knowledge needed to create healthier, more fulfilling relationships.

Reflecting on your journey also involves recognizing that healing is a lifelong process. Attachment healing is not something that happens overnight, nor is it a destination that you reach and then move on from. It is an ongoing process that requires continuous effort, self-awareness, and growth. As you continue on this path, you will encounter new challenges and opportunities for growth. There may be times when old patterns resurface, or when you find yourself struggling with insecurity or fear. These moments are not signs of failure but are instead opportunities to deepen your understanding and strengthen your commitment to healing.

The lifelong process of attachment healing involves maintaining the practices and strategies you have learned throughout this journey. It means continuing to engage in self-reflection, regularly assessing your thoughts, feelings, and behaviors to ensure that you are staying aligned with your goals. It means practicing mindfulness, self-care, and emotional regulation, using these tools to navigate life's challenges with resilience and grace. It also means remaining open to change, being willing to adapt and grow as you continue to evolve. Healing is not a linear process; it is a dynamic journey that ebbs and flows, requiring patience, persistence, and self-compassion.

As you move forward, it is essential to surround yourself with support. Whether it is through close relationships, therapy, or support groups, having a network of people who understand your journey and can offer encouragement is invaluable. These connections provide a sense of security and belonging, helping you stay grounded and motivated as you continue to heal. They also serve as a reminder that you are not alone on this journey, that others have walked this path before you and that you have the strength and resilience to continue.

Final thoughts on this journey emphasize the importance of self-compassion and kindness. Healing from insecure attachment is a deeply personal and often challenging process, and it is crucial to treat yourself with the same kindness and understanding that you would offer to a loved one. There will be moments of doubt, frustration, and even setbacks, but it is in these moments that self-compassion becomes most important. Remind yourself that you are doing the best you can and that every step you take, no matter how small, is a step toward healing and growth. Celebrate your progress, acknowledge your efforts, and be patient with yourself as you continue to evolve.

In offering encouragement, it is important to remember that this journey is one of transformation and empowerment. The work you have done to understand and heal your attachment style is not just about improving your relationships; it is about reclaiming your sense of self, building your emotional resilience, and creating a life that is fulfilling and meaningful. You have taken the first steps toward a more secure and balanced life, and with each step, you are moving closer to the life you desire. The journey may be long, and the path may be challenging, but the rewards; greater self-awareness, healthier relationships, and a deeper sense of peace, are worth every effort.

As you conclude this exploration, know that you have the power to shape your future. The knowledge, tools, and insights you have gained are now part of your journey, guiding you as you continue to grow and heal. Embrace the process, stay committed to your path, and trust that you are capable of creating the secure, fulfilling life you deserve. This is not the end of your journey, but rather a new beginning, one where you move forward with confidence, resilience, and a deep sense of self-love and compassion.